A
MODEST
PROPOSAL

To solve the Palestine-Israel conflict

Karl Sabbagh

SKYSCRAPER

Published by Skyscraper Publications Limited
20 Crab Tree Close, Bloxham, Oxon OX15 4SE
www.skyscraperpublications.com
First published 2018

Copyright© 2018 Karl Sabbagh

Cover concept and design by Rebecca Lynch

Printed in the United Kingdom by CPI
ISBN-13: 978-1-911072-26-3

The Title

The phrase "A Modest Proposal" has been used generically to describe what has been called "a straight-faced satire." The first "modest proposal" was Jonathan Swift's suggestion, published anonymously, that poverty could be relieved in Ireland by poor people selling their children as food for rich people.

I am perhaps laying myself open to the charge that this short book is itself a satire, because it may be seen as "using exaggeration to expose and criticize people's vices, particularly in the context of contemporary politics", one definition of satire.

But in fact, there is irony too in Swift's use of the title. Far from being 'modest' in the sense that I might say 'it will take a modest amount of effort' to do something, this book proposes a solution to the Palestine-Israel conflict which is about as immodest as you could get – it will require a huge amount of effort, collaboration, fund-raising and organisation to achieve it. But in my view – and that of an increasing number of informed observers of the Middle East – it may be the only solution that will actually work by bringing peace to the region after a hundred years of mismanagement, cowardice, wishful thinking, and prejudice.

What this book may do is perhaps force people to say "Well, if not this, then what?" Because the one thing that cannot be denied is the right of people to live in the homeland from which they have been expelled. If that right is not achievable for the Palestinians by my "modest proposal" for a single state between the Jordan and the Mediterranean, combined with the right of return for Palestinians, what other option is there?

Karl Sabbagh
February 2018

Table of Contents

Introduction

I have visited Palestine and Israel on many occasions over the last fifty years. I think I know quite a lot about the history of the region and the people who live there. But every visit has taught me something new. This book really crystallized on a visit I made in May 2016, to attend the opening of the Palestinian Museum near Ramallah on the West Bank. For some years, I have been a supporter of the One Democratic State idea, for reasons which I will describe in more detail in Chapter 7. This foresees the only just solution of the Palestine-Israel dispute as being a single state between the Jordan river and the Mediterranean, taking in all of Israel, the West Bank, and Gaza.

For people who have never visited the area, the words 'Israel' and 'Palestine' (these days, the West Bank and Gaza) probably conjure up images of two very different territories: one cosmopolitan, 'civilised', democratic, a member of the world community of developed states, inhabited by an ancient people who have made a major contribution to world civilisation, and the other rural, poor, peasant-oriented, dusty, uncontrollable, governed by terrorists or at least by people who are perpetually angry, and with little or no cultural heritage beyond hummus and folk-dancing. To merge the two might seem to present the same problems as combining East and West Germany.

Seen like this, who could possibly disagree that the best solution would be a compete separation between the two territories, rather than any attempt to mix the two, which would be like mixing oil and water. (In passing – and irrelevantly – the Israelis wish they had oil, and keep taking the Palestinians' water.)

In fact, the characterisation I have just described is a false one. Israel is becoming the uncontrollable one, with an increasingly racist government whose racism is directed as much against its poor Jewish inhabitants as against Palestinian Arabs. It is a country in the thrall of religious extremism, to the extent that secular Jews face all sorts of illiberal laws, from the trivial – lifts which are switched off on Fridays – to laws governing birth, marriage and death which are an affront to the civil liberties of at least half its inhabitants. Few of its Jewish inhabitants can trace any link with the country going back more than a couple of generations, and it doesn't even have a convenient rail service between its two biggest cities, Jerusalem and Tel Aviv. Palestine, on the other hand, has the highest proportion of graduates in the Middle East, a thriving society rooted in centuries of continuity of family habitation in the same towns and villages, an intellectual heritage which made possible the development of Western culture, and a cuisine which clearly strikes Jewish Israelis as better than Jewish food since they keep claiming it as their own.

It was two meals during my May visit which brought home what One Democratic State might actually look like, or rather feel like. On the day of the opening of the Museum, a group of us were driven off to a village nearby for lunch. The food was beautifully cooked, the place was full and the conversation animated. The clientele were unremarkable, middle class, some formally dressed, others in casual clothes; a range of ages and – as far as I could infer – professions. There was a formality about some of the diners.

Like me, they had been to a celebration, the opening of a new museum, but otherwise they could have been members of any middle class in any country. We sat outside, under awnings, and were served by smartly-dressed waiters. The conversation with Palestinians was wide-ranging, covering the political situation, certainly, but other topics too. And, unlike the situation that might apply in a good restaurant in the West, the food was exactly the range of dishes you might expect to find on a domestic Palestinian dinner table with ingredients all probably from the nearby land – the village was surrounded by an undulating landscape with olive groves, orchards, and fields of sheep.

Twenty-four hours later, after a short untroubled journey of 70 kilometres or so in a taxi, I was having another meal in Israel, in the town of Jaffa, now a suburb of Tel Aviv and formerly one of the leading Arab towns of pre-1948 Palestine. When I say 'untroubled' I should say that it was untroubled for me, when it is likely to have been a very troubled journey – if not impossible – for certain classes of Palestinian.

I had been thinking a lot that week about the idea of a single democratic state in the territory between the Jordan river and the Mediterranean, and one question suddenly arose in my mind. If that single democratic state were to come into being – in the teeth of objections by the current Israeli government – what would be different about these two days and these two social occasions? I could think of nothing. The restaurants would still exist, where they were. The cuisines would still be similar. (That night in Jaffa I had well-prepared *mansaf*, an Arab dish.) The range of people in the restaurants would be similar. I would have travelled between the two places in a modern taxi or bus, on well-constructed roads, and found my way back to a comfortable hotel. The only difference I could think of was that – in the new One-State, the first restaurant would have Jews among the customers, whereas at the moment Jews – apart from the illegal settlers – are discouraged from travelling into the Occupied Territories. And in the second restaurant there would perhaps have been more Arabs, although since Jaffa was originally an Arab town I'm sure there was a sprinkling the night I was there.

And that insight raised another issue. Looking at the customers in both restaurants, I would not have the faintest idea who was an Arab and who a Jew. The range of facial types among each ethnic group made it impossible to identify anyone as unambiguously a Jew or an Arab if they were not wearing characteristic headwear.

There was no obvious transition between the two territories on my journey, other than the point at which we drove without stopping through a checkpoint at the notorious Wall, and not much difference in the experiences at either end. The buildings seen on the way were similar – neat, regimented Jewish housing alternating with more traditional stone Arab villages, in both territories; good quality highways with worse minor roads, in both territories; buses plying their routes, similar-looking soldiers and police, in different uniforms; mobile phone reception, and so on. There were even pockets of poverty in both territories – refugee camps in one; Oriental Jews herded into poor housing in the other.

I am not trying to say that the two communities could be welded seamlessly into one, if the whole area became a single state. Nevertheless, for me that trip presented a vision of what a single state might be like. On the ground, it seems eminently possible. Comparing it with German reunification, paradoxically it is Israel's increasing grip on Palestinian areas that would make such a change easier. Roads, water systems, communications, the media, all share systems in a way which the two Germanys never did. I made a television documentary about the problems of reuniting the two halves of Berlin after 1989, and from railways which changed gauge at the border to incompatible telephones and sewage systems, the problems were far greater than the technical problems of reuniting the Occupied Territories and Israel.

One other benefit of visiting Israel and Palestine over the years is an appreciation of the landscape. There's a lot of it. Again, to return to our uninformed observer, she is sometimes given the impression that Israel is packed to the gunwales, a densely-populated state with no room for the millions of Palestinians who would claim the right to return in any peace settlement. In fact, the state houses about 370 people per square kilometre, nowhere near the top of the world population density league. And any protestation that there is no room for more people is nullified by the fact that Israel issues an open invitation to any Jew in the world – all fifteen million of them outside Israel by its own legal definition – to come and live there, with no mention of possible overcrowding as a problem. It is the availability of this space that leads me to the second theme of this book – a plan for the right of return. This is usually presented in a context determined by Israel and its perceived needs (or wishes). Successive Israeli governments have resolutely refused to consider the idea that any Palestinians or their descendants would ever be allowed to return to their ancestral land. In fact, they even block Palestinians from visiting Israel today. Since a Two-State Solution is the only proposal that Israel has ever even paid lip service to, 'peace' discussions of the right of return – when it has been considered at all – have been confined to the logistics of returning Palestinians to 18 percent of the Palestine from which they were expelled, rather than the entire area, which is my proposal in this book.

When all citizens of the new state can drive from Jaffa to Ramallah for lunch, or the reverse, with no checkpoints, no showing of identity cards, no 'security wall', and a sense of identity with a constitution which gives everyone exactly the same rights of residence, religion (or none) and representation in government, the Israel-Palestine conflict will be over, and the sum total of justice and freedom for all its citizens will be greater than it has been for any of them and their ancestors for the last hundred years.

One final point: in 1902 a novel was published, *Altneuland*, or 'Old New Land', which described a Jewish state in Palestine, at a time when there were barely 22,000 Jews in the country, compared with 554,000 Arabs. It was written by Theodore Herzl, one of the founders of Zionism, the philosophy that the Jews of the world should have a state of their own. At the time he wrote the book, I wonder if he saw it as a blueprint for what might actually happen, in the face of the overwhelming improbability that a small subset of politically motivated Jews would get rid of most of the majority population who were not Jews and be allowed to call the country their own? I suspect not, just as I have to confess that I don't see the plan outlined in this book being achieved overnight or without huge unforeseeable actions taking place on the world stage to achieve it. But that's what happened with Herzl's vision, and perhaps it could happen with mine.

Part 1
The Background

—

1 The transformation of Palestine

There are about twelve million Palestinians in the world, about six million living outside pre-1948 Palestine. This is a figure that chimes uncomfortably with the figure of six million Jews who died at the hands of the Nazis. Sadly, the two figures are not entirely unconnected. Without a massive wave of sympathy for the plight of the surviving Jews after World War II, it is unlikely that a UN vote would have been passed – by a very narrow margin – that unilaterally handed over large areas of Palestine, more than half, to a population of largely European Jews whose right to take over the Arab land of Palestine was tenuous, to put it at its strongest. This in turn led to the deliberate expulsion of many of the indigenous inhabitants of Palestine and the destruction or theft of their homes, property and livelihoods.

The number of Palestinians expelled or killed was something short of a million, 50% of the entire Arab population of Palestine at the time. It is they and their descendants who make up today's Palestinians, and nothing has happened in the intervening years to negate their claim to the land from which they were expelled.

The Zionist politicians who planned the dispossession of the Palestinians over the thirty years from 1918 to 1948 held two beliefs that showed that they had profoundly misjudged the situation. The first was the belief that they could ultimately acquire all of Palestine between the Jordan river and the Mediterranean for themselves, by pretending to accept less to start with. The second was that they would be able to achieve a quick and effective expulsion of all Palestinians from their homeland and then, after the event, the dispossessed Palestinians or at least their children and grandchildren, would soon accept the loss of their land and make new homes wherever they had ended up.

These two fateful misjudgements led to consequences which reached beyond the immediate confines of the small state of Palestine and its neighbours.

The first decision – to use the area of Palestine allotted to the Jews by the UN as a springboard to take over the areas allotted to the Arabs – has been the cause of three wars and innumerable incursions and acts of occupation.

Every major aggressive act by Israel since 1948 has been carried out in order to grab more land and expand Israel towards a takeover of the entire land of Palestine, or to kill or expel Palestinians who unaccountably – to the Israelis – persist in seeing the theft of their land as a live issue and one that must eventually be resolved with justice.

Israel has tried for years to maintain with a straight face that its aggression against Palestinian lands and the Palestinian people is merely a matter of protecting its existence.

But many Israeli historians, with access to the national archives and the increasing availability of formerly secret documents, now accept that what the Palestinians have been saying for decades is true – that there was a deliberate plan before and after 1948 to kill or expel Palestinians and take over their land and property, and that every Israeli government since has had as an unstated aim the eventual acquisition by force if necessary of the rest of Palestine.

It did not need to be like this. Jews and Arabs had lived peaceably in Palestine for centuries. My own family, like every Arab family who lived in a mixed Arab-Jewish area of Palestine, had Jewish friends with whom they shared meals or picnics or baby-sitting or shopping. In the years up to 1917 – the point at which the British government allied itself with the views of those Jews who wanted to take over Palestine – Jews never made up more than 10% of the population, but they were not in any sense a deprived or suppressed minority. Antisemitism was largely a product of the West rather than of the Arab world. At various points during the 1920s and 1930s, the Zionist Jews who were pushing the British to give them more and more say in the running of the country always said – in public – that their vision was of a shared state, in which Jewish intelligence and resources could help to raise the standard of living for all inhabitants of Palestine, Jews and Arabs, Christians and Muslims.

In fact, there is ample evidence that, in private, Zionists were saying the opposite, that in the end, the Palestinians would have to accept a Jewish state replacing what was currently an Arab one.

The British Jewish writer, Israel Zangwill, wrote:

> We cannot allow the Arabs to block so valuable a piece of historic reconstruction ... And therefore we must generally persuade them to 'trek.' There is no particular reason for the Arabs to cling to these few kilometers. 'To fold their tents and silently steal away' is their proverbial habit: let them exemplify it now.

A Zionist who became Chief Political Officer of Palestine, Richard Meinertzhagen, wrote in his diary:

> I personally am prepared to back Jew against Arab every time. The Jew means progress ... the Arab is stagnation and stands for immorality, rotten government, corrupt and dishonest society.

And Chaim Weizmann, the Zionist who persuaded the

British government to support a Jewish state in Palestine made similarly racist remarks when he wrote:

> [The indigenous population is akin to] the rocks of Judea, as obstacles that have to be cleared on a difficult path.

By the early 1940s, with illegal immigration on the increase and clear evidence that the British had no power to stop the bulk of it, there was little doubt in Palestinian minds about the way things were going.

By this stage, the plight of European Jewry was becoming clear, and the Zionists were able to paint a picture of thousands of Jews desperate to go to Palestine. In fact, many of them were desperate to go anywhere but Palestine, a hot, dusty, unfamiliar Middle Eastern country with which they had nothing in common. But the USA and Canada – where many wanted to go – closed their doors, and even attempts made by the British to house Jewish orphans were thwarted by the Zionists for whom all Jews – including children – must go to Palestine whether they wanted to or not.

The view expressed by David Ben Gurion in 1938 leaves no doubt about the Zionists' priorities:

> If I knew that it would be possible to save all the children in Germany by bringing them over to England, and only half by transporting to Eretz Yisrael [the Land of Israel], then I would opt for the second alternative. For we must weigh not only the life of these children, but also the history of the People of Israel.

All of this could have triggered a vicious anti-Zionist terrorist resistance by Palestinian Arabs, still a majority in their own country, but somehow they had faith that the British, still in control of the country, would not let them down.

In fact, the terrorism was largely on the other side, carried out in a decade-long campaign by Jewish terror groups, aided by the official Jewish militias, whose anger was directed at the indigenous Arabs who persisted in seeking to live in and govern their own land.

Even in 1946, when things started to fall apart, and after many hundreds of Arab civilians had been killed by Jewish terrorism, the Arab League – on behalf of the Palestinian Arabs who had no official voice in the growing search for a solution – offered a form of government which would be shared by all the inhabitants of Palestine. According to the New York Times:

> The plan contemplates a transition period during which a Government of Arabs and Zionists would be appointed by the British mandatory authorities to draft the Constitution and arrange for the election of the assembly. ... The Zionists would be represented in the provisional government and in the various branches of the subsequent permanent government in proportion to their strength among the legal residents of Palestine.

Many Arabs by this time had come to accept that the Jewish inhabitants of Palestine, still less than half the population in spite of massive immigration, some of it illegal, could not and should not leave. Not because the Jews had a legal claim to the land but because this was one way of solving an intractable problem that had been on the world stage for three decades and which they saw as likely to continue in a way which could only cause further harm to the Arabs of Palestine. These Arabs were entitled to – and had been promised – self-determination in their own land but had seen the successive erosion of their own rights to a point where they appeared to be in danger of losing that land. The offer to share was partly magnanimous and partly pragmatic. The Arab-Zionist Palestine that would have emerged from the proposal involved a genuine sharing of government, land and rights. It would have been One Democratic State of Palestine, a phrase which seventy years later, and abbreviated to ODS, has gained currency as all other solutions to the Arab-Israel conflict seem farther away than ever.

This 1946 plan did not happen, of course. It was rejected

out of hand by the Zionists. Instead, with no thought for the consequences of their actions, the Zionists spent the years from 1946 to 1948 accelerating a policy which explicitly aimed to deprive Palestinians of their land and their rights. It was a two-pronged policy. One prong was to make life as difficult as possible in Palestine, for the Arabs, the British – now the Zionists' enemy – and any Jews who disagreed with the aim of an exclusively Jewish state. The other was to run a campaign of misinformation, bribery, threats and exploitation of guilt in the West that smeared arguments on behalf of the Palestinians as motivated by antisemitism and a callous disregard for the plight of Holocaust victims, and tried to make sure that players on the world stage, principally through the United Nations, gave their support to the mission to hand Palestine over to the Jews.

Looking back at this campaign, and its continuation in another form once the state of Israel was established, it is clear today that in any modern solution to the Palestine-Israel issue there is an imbalance of responsibility. This is rarely acknowledged, by anyone apart from supporters of the Palestinians, and never by Jewish Israelis. But that fact forms a background to this book. Up till now, any proposed 'solution' to the conflict has been presented as one in which each side has to compromise in its aims, as if each side was equally to blame. I do not take that view. As I said in 2006 in my book *Palestine: A Personal History:*

> The fact is the Palestinians did nothing to cause their own fate. Did the Palestinians slaughter and expel themselves? Did they compel Jews from Europe to flock to Palestine and buy up land? Did the Palestinians lobby the British government to give away a land that didn't belong to them? Obviously, few politicians in Israel today were directly involved in the takeover of Palestine (although Sharon was, as were most of the early Israeli Prime Ministers). And Israelis living in a fashionable house formerly owned by an Arab family are not directly responsible for the theft of that house. But they should at least accept that its original

inhabitants are absent not by choice, but because they were brutally expelled.

The plan I present in this book shows how, by combining two proposals, each of which has been part of a separate plan for a resolution of the conflict, a solution which might have seemed fanciful, unachievable and even unfair comes into focus as by far the fairest to all parties. This does not necessarily make it achievable, but so far, in a hundred years of peace-making attempts, there has not been one solution proposed that in any sense at all has been fair to the Palestinians, so fairness to the Palestinians – without a huge injustice to the Jewish inhabitants of Israel – is at least halfway towards the objective. I also believe that when reasonable people see the net value of the solution to both parties in the conflict they may no longer accept the decades of tendentious and malicious propaganda that has been presented to the world by Israel and its supporters in an attempt to quash any consideration of the rights of the Palestinians.

What is the 'solution' I am offering and which I explore in more detail in this book? It is based on two principles which have often been considered separately in recent years but which, in combination, could overcome a number of objections which have been presented to each.

The first is the principle that there should be one democratic state of all its inhabitants between the Jordan river and the Mediterranean. There are two unsurprising things about this idea. One is that this is what Palestine should have become after the First World War if the principles applied to other former Ottoman Empire states had been respected in the post-War peace treaties. The other unsurprising thing is that this definition is merely restating a principle that applies to democratic nations throughout the world. All the citizens of nations within specific boundaries have the right to share in a democratic government which runs that nation. Of course, there are some nations where geography and social or ethnic divisions interact, and this leads to a more nuanced form of government, although still one in which, in principle, individual

23

communities should not be disadvantaged compared with others. But the enlarged state between the Jordan and the Mediterranean would not be such a territory. In pre-Mandate Palestine and even in Palestine under the British Mandate, there were not areas that were exclusively Jewish or exclusively Arab. Of course, there were towns, villages and other communities which had a predominance of one or other religious group, but it was never the case that those groups had different rights, until in the later years of the Mandate the British gave in to Jewish demands for special treatment. Today, of course, in modern Israel there are all sorts of restrictions enshrined in law which discriminate against one group of citizens – Palestinian Arab citizens of Israel – in favour of another – Israeli Jews. (It's worth saying here that anti-Arab discrimination is not the only form of discrimination practised officially in Israel. Many non-religious Israeli Jews feel that they too are subject to restrictive laws drawn up under pressure from the religious authorities to favour those who practice Judaism over those who don't.)

The second principle which is at the core of a future solution is the right of return for Palestinian Arabs. It is enshrined in UN Resolution 194, passed within seven months of the establishment of Israel. Among its clauses is one that calls for refugees to be allowed to return to their homeland or for compensation to be paid for loss of property by the government responsible.

Of course, the landscape – literally and metaphorically – has changed over the last seventy years and the right of return I shall describe in detail in Chapter 8 reflects that change. When this topic is discussed, all sorts of issues are raised about who should return and where they should go, as well as, in the case of compensation, what should it be *for,* how should it be calculated, and who should pay it, and I will enlarge on all these issues.

But the argument at the heart of my book, an argument which has some new aspects to it and which certainly bears serious consideration, is that the combination of a single state of Jews and Arabs and a proper, thought-through, well-funded right of return overcomes objections which have been raised to each of these suggestions separately.

To give one example: The illegal Israeli settlements have been a stumbling block in any negotiations between Israelis and Palestinians over the Two-State Proposal. The Palestinians have insisted that any territory provided for a Palestinian state should be free of these illegal settlements. The Israelis have insisted that provision should be made to retain the major settlement blocks. And indeed, the previous attempts that have been made to remove tiny settlements, barely huts or caravans, have been manipulated for publicity purposes by ultra-right-wing Jews so as to make it clear that with the best will in the world – which the Israeli government certainly does not demonstrate – the dismantling of the large towns that have been established on Palestinian land would be a major task and could well result in a civil war in Israel. It would also be very costly. Removing a block of settlements in Gaza in 2005, with about 8,000 residents, cost the Israeli government over $2 billion. Pro rata, to remove 500,000 settlers from the West Bank would cost $62 billion.

But suppose the whole area of the West Bank, Israel and Gaza was one state under one government of all its inhabitants? In a sense, the West Bank would no longer be 'occupied'. The status of settlements would be no different from the status of any town or village elsewhere in the area of the new state. Or rather, the status of those settlements would have to *become* no different.

Further, the new merging of the Occupied Territories and Israel would remove obstacles to the exercise of the right of return. Up till now, with control of Israel in the hands of the Jewish government, all discussion of where Palestinians would return to has concentrated on the West Bank. Any return to territory in what is now Israel has been rejected out of hand. Of course, this makes a nonsense of the whole idea of 'return'. For a family from a village in the Galilee to return to a house in Jericho, say, would be no return at all, merely exchanging one foreign residence for another, even if, for a family from a Lebanese refugee camp this would have some benefits. What is needed – and just – is a genuine, well-motivated, well-funded right of *real* return, to a location which is at least in the vicinity of the ancestral home. This means that families from villages in the Galilee or southern Israel could return to those areas, rather than being herded into the West Bank. And of course, since it is likely that some at least of the Israeli West Bank settlers, who are characterised by a racist attitude to Arabs, might well seek to return to where *they* came from – Brooklyn or North London, say – there would be empty houses in the now unsegregated settlements, to which some Palestinians could return.

The above is just one example of the synergy that could arise from a combination of the one-state solution and the right of return for Palestinians. I hope to show in the rest of the book how there are many examples – and many advantages – from this new approach.

2 The Three Pillars of Injustice

There are three elements which underlie and support the Palestinian need for justice. The Old Testament Book of Proverbs speaks of Wisdom as a house "built on Seven Pillars". We could well speak of Injustice, in the case of the Palestinians, as built on Three Pillars. These are:

- The pseudo-legal justification, largely facilitated by the British with help from the USA over the years from 1917 to 1947, for turning a large area of Palestine into a Jewish state.
- The military campaign from 1947-49 designed to extend the initial boundaries of that state into Palestinian areas and to expel Palestinians from historic Palestine.
- The promotion of wars and conflict in the Middle East from 1949 to the present day to complete the takeover and dispossess or expel more Palestinians.

Let's take these in turn:
As part of a peace treaty between Turkey and the

victorious allies after the First World War, Britain sought and was granted control over an area of the Middle East known as Palestine. At the time, Palestine covered an area which the Ottoman (Turkish) government had divided into several provinces, but for centuries, partly because of its significance for three world religions, inhabitants and visitors knew the area as 'Palestine', with Jerusalem as its capital.

The people who lived in Palestine were mainly Arabs, with a small proportion, less than ten percent, of Jews. Some of these Arabs were descended from people who had lived in the area for many centuries, stretching back to the Canaanites, whom ancient Israel tried to exterminate. What is certainly the case is that when 20th century Jewish claims to Palestine started to be made, the people who made these claims, known as political Zionists, had no demonstrable connection with Palestine, other than a diffuse religious-cultural association and a desire to take it over. Whereas the indigenous Arab people who lived there when these claims were being made could trace their ancestors back many generations, through carefully preserved family trees and an intimate knowledge of the villages and towns in which previous generations had lived.

This difference – between people in Europe who claimed the right to own the land, but who had no personal connection with it, and the inhabitants who were rooted culturally and socially in the land – cannot be emphasised too strongly and too often, because it explains the unwillingness of Palestinians in the first few years of British rule to believe for a moment that their land might one day be taken away from them, with British collusion, and given to an alien group of largely European Jews.

But taken away it was, in the following manner:

A letter, signed by a British Foreign Secretary, Arthur Balfour, under pressure from Jewish colleagues and a small group of political Zionist Jews in Britain, was published in November 1917. This was the famous (or infamous) Balfour Declaration. It wasn't really much of a 'declaration,' more a mild expression of support. In the letter, Balfour tells Lord

Rothschild that the British government 'views with favour' the establishment of a Jewish national home in Palestine, rather in the way you might 'view with favour' the establishment of an old folks' home at the end of your road. In neither case are you committed to support the home with every fibre of your being, in the teeth of the people who live on the site already.

There are many odd things about this letter and the significance it was soon to assume. First, although it was issued in the name of the Cabinet, there were a lot of other things going on at the time – World War 1 for example – which meant that nobody, apart from Balfour and his ally in the matter, the Prime Minister Lloyd George, paid it much attention. The topic of the Balfour Declaration was the last item on an agenda with eleven other items including such important matters as air raids and food supplies, activity on the Western front, and the invasion of Italy.[1]

Indeed, this is what one cabinet member was reported as saying about the letter, looking back at it a few years later:

At the time the policy was first taken over by the Cabinet, this was done with altogether insufficient consideration. Mr. Lloyd George had insisted on the necessity for winning over Jewish-American influences in the United States to the side of the Allies by a measure installing Zionism in Palestine. This measure was accepted hastily, every member of the Cabinet being intensely preoccupied with his own share of the prosecution of the War. There was no proper consideration of previous countervailing pledges to the Arabs, no proper realization of the moral necessity of consulting the population of Palestine upon their fate, no proper understanding of the emptiness of the safeguards in the 'Balfour Declaration' so far as that population was concerned.

---

[1] *Anglo-Arab Relations and the Question of Palestine*, 1914-21, A.L. Tibawi, Luzac, 1977 pp 232-33

This cabinet member was Edwin Montagu, a Jew who was quite happy to be British and objected to the idea put about by the group behind the Balfour Declaration that Jews needed a state of their own to be fully Jewish. He objected even more to the fact that the Zionists were acting as if the state they claimed was uninhabited when in fact it had an indigenous Arab population which was more entitled to the land than European Jews.

Another odd thing, as *Daily Mail* journalist J.M.N. Jeffries pointed out, was that the organisation of the letter and much of the wording came not from the British government but from a group of Zionists, both from Britain and elsewhere in Europe, organised by Chaim Weizmann, a Russian Jew, and with Lord Rothschild as a supporter and figurehead. As Jeffries wrote:

> The walls of the Foreign Office without doubt have enclosed many a singular scene, but they might well have inclined together to hide from view the spectacle of a Secretary of State asking a visitor from Russia to give him a draft of his own Cabinet's measures.

Equally strange was the fact that a letter was delivered to Rothschild by the British government of whose contents he was only too aware because he helped to write it.

And strangest of all is the way in which, in spite of the fact that it was just a letter of encouragement, within a few years it had assumed the status of an unbreakable treaty, although who the second party was, along with the British government, was unclear. This is an important point. In later years, the Balfour Declaration was taken to be an unbreakable promise by Britain to the Jews of the world. But the Jews of the world were not a treaty-making body.

They were a religious or ethnic or social group, like the Catholics of the world or the redheads of the world or the vegetarians of the world.

What's more, there is no evidence that the Jews of the world, as a body, even wanted to go and live in Palestine.

Certainly, there were protests among many British Jews when the Balfour Declaration was published, because they felt that their national identity was British and that the eventual existence of a Jewish state would mean that Jews throughout the world would have an alien nationality imposed on them when they were quite happy as they were, thank you very much.

Nevertheless, in the months and years after the end of the First World War, the Zionists took every opportunity to use the Balfour Declaration as a lever to remind the British government that it had promised Palestine to the Jews. So much so that the British government even began to believe it.

The crucial transformation from 'just a letter' to treaty status occurred during Peace Treaty discussions dealing with what was to happen to the Ottoman Empire, now that the imperialist Turks who had ruled Palestine were defeated. Britain had all sorts of interests in the Middle East that led its leaders to want to control parts of the former Ottoman Empire.

Some were strategic, to do with commanding routes to their major imperial possession, India; others were economic – there had already been substantial discoveries of oil in various parts of the world, and the significance of controlling other people's oil became clear during the First World War when the British navy had an insatiable thirst for the fuel.

The discussions over how to carve up the post-war Middle East were bedevilled by interstate rivalries, principally the competing claims of Britain and France to Syria, Palestine and Mesopotamia (later Iraq). With lots of backstairs dealings, Britain obtained what was called a 'mandate' for Palestine, granted by the newly formed League of Nations. There were certain rules laid down for the operation of these mandates.

One of them was the requirement for the mandatory power to usher the inhabitants of the country towards eventual self-government.

This happened in Iraq for example, also under Britain. But in the British mandate for Palestine, the vital clause was negated by the inclusion of the Balfour Declaration which required the mandatory power to facilitate the establishment of a Jewish National Home in Palestine.

As with the Balfour Declaration, the Zionists who had drafted it played a large part in the wording of the Mandate. The group of Zionists who drafted the Balfour Declaration tried to insert a phrase about "reconstituting" Palestine as a Jewish state. Historically this was a nonsense. As George Curzon, who succeeded Balfour as Foreign Secretary, wrote:

> I do not ... recognise that the connection of the Jews with Palestine, which terminated 1200 years ago, gives them any claims whatsoever. On this principle we have a stronger claim to France.

It is worth diverging for a moment to explore this point in a little detail. There is such a strong belief among today's Jews – and the non-Jews who have been exposed to pro-Israel arguments – that they are in some sense the true inheritors of Palestine, that it seems perverse to deny it. For many people, even some supporters of Palestinian rights, Palestine "used to be a Jewish state." The argument for them is not over that point but addresses a different issue – whether the descendants of citizens of a state which existed 2000 years ago have any claim on it today. But if you look at the history of Jews in Palestine, the story is more complex.

The Judeans, whose name evolved to the word Jews, lived in the province of Judah from about the 6th century BC, under the Babylonians, the Persians, the Ptolemies and the Seleucids.

There were other provinces in what became Palestine. These were Idumea, Galilee, Gaumantis, Samaria, Decapolis, and provinces which bordered these provinces but extended north or east beyond Palestine.

There were therefore all sorts of other tribal groups living outside Judea who, if we could identify their descendants today, could lay equal claim to Palestine (equally illogically). Indeed, there is stronger evidence that many of today's Palestinian Arabs are descended from the occupants of parts of Palestine 2,500 years ago, than that many of today's Jews are.

In the 130s BC, the Hasmonean Hyrcanus I, a Judean, conquered the whole of Palestine. There was a population of about a million, but although they were under a Jewish king they were not all ethnically Jewish. Indeed, again, some were the ancestors of the Palestinian Arabs.

Probably less than half the population was ethnically Jewish and at that point the only sense in which the rest of the inhabitants were Jewish was a political, religious or cultural one, rather as we used to think of Russians as communists.

To add to the confusion, Israel ("Eretz Israel") was the term applied to the territory of Samaria, north of Judea, and the Judeans ("Jews") adopted membership of "Israel" in the 6th century. But the Samaritans, as they were called by the Jews, called themselves Israelites and not Jews.

What this all means, to oversimply a bit, is that there was never an ethnically Jewish state of Palestine. There was certainly a state of Palestine under a Jewish king, many of whose inhabitants may have practiced the Jewish religion. After revolting against the Romans, the Jews in Palestine were largely expelled and spread out over other countries around the Mediterranean. Modern Jews, and Zionists in particular, base their claims on some assumed *ethnic* continuity between Palestine 2500 years ago, and today.

But even if it was possible to demonstrate a link between modern Jews and those original communities, this could only apply to one group of Jews, those called Sephardi Jews who coalesced in the Iberian peninsula, Spain and Portugal, in the early Middle Ages. In the 20th century, there were small communities of Sephardic Jews in Palestine, and there still are.

Interestingly, they tend to be non-Zionist, happy to live in Eretz Israel and practice their religion but with no particular attachment to an ethnically Jewish state.

The Jews in Europe and America who were and are most vociferous in claiming Palestine as a Jewish state are from another group, called Ashkenazi Jews. These emerged in

Europe at the end of the first millennium. Some historians[2] and geneticists believe they had no connection with the Jews who lived in Palestine but were the descendants of a nation called the Khazars, situated between the Black Sea and the Caspian Sea, who converted to Judaism in the 8th or 9th centuries. On that basis, even if one felt that people whose ancestors lived in a land 2000 years ago should be allowed to colonise it today, the Ashkenazim are disqualified. Many Jewish historians and scientists dispute this finding, but, as with Jewish archaeologists (see later), some Jewish historians and scientists see their main role in life as refuting any data that are critical of their particular view of the Jews.

Even in the absence of an ethnic justification, it is possible for religious Jews to claim Palestine solely on religious grounds, ("given to the Jews by God"), but even if there were any validity in such a claim, it would not apply to the many secular Jews around the world, probably more than half, whom God would surely have excluded from his gift if he'd been able to contemplate such an oddity as a secular Jew.

I have gone into this detail, not because I think that if there were a genetic link between today's Jews and the inhabitants of 1st century Palestine it would have the slightest relevance to the political situation today, but because it has become received opinion that such a link is somehow a justification to ethically cleanse Palestine of its indigenous population.

So back to the Balfour Declaration and the Mandate.

The phrase "National Home" in the Balfour Declaration and the Mandate was a phrase which was chosen so as not to alarm the Arabs about the true intentions of Britain and the Zionists. There were many public denials by leading British statesmen that the intention was to turn Palestine into a Jewish state, but in private, the Zionist leader Chaim Weizmann said the phrase meant that Palestine should become "a state as Jewish as England is English". Furthermore, by some sleight

[2]See Shlomo Sand, *The Invention of the Jewish People*, Verso, 2010

of hand or other, the Zionists led by Weizmann, who were constantly in attendance on any occasion when the future of Palestine was discussed or documents drafted, managed to get inserted into the Mandate a key phrase which the Foreign Office had struck out of drafts of the Balfour Declaration. It was important to the Zionists to persuade the world that there was a historical connection between the Jews of Palestine and modern Jews, even though there is no evidence for this. The drafters of the Mandate had agreed to insert a phrase about "recognising the historic connection" of the Jewish people with Palestine, but that wasn't good enough, and pressure was exerted to change that to "reconstituting their national home," as if it had ever been constituted in the first place, other than in a religious sense rather than an ethnic one.

As these documents went through their several drafts, there were one or two civil servants in the Foreign Office who had more grasp of the true situation in Palestine than Balfour and Lloyd George. One of them, Alfred Milner, was very aware that the country was full of Arabs and inserted in the Balfour Declaration the phrase "it being clearly understood that nothing shall be done to prejudice the civil and religious rights of the existing non-Jewish communities in Palestine."

Milner didn't go as far as to call them 'Arabs' but even this phrase angered Lord Rothschild, who saw the inclusion of this phrase as 'a slur on Zionism'.

The 'non-Jewish communities in Palestine' were actually 90% of the population, Muslim and Christian Arabs, and as the years passed under British control, no one in the government paid more than lip service to this proviso. Indeed, the very fact that Jews from round the world with no connection with Palestine were given special treatment embodied in the laws of Palestine was, by definition, prejudicing the civil, religious (and political) rights of Palestine's 'non-Jewish' inhabitants.

There is almost no more to be said to explain how today's Palestinians came to be scattered over the world, deprived of their homes and sometimes their lives. From the beginning of British control of Palestine to the end, the British facilitated – or at least colluded in – the mass immigration of Jews to Palestine, as part of the process envisaged by the Zionists and accepted by many British politicians, to increase the Jewish population of Palestine until the Jews were in a majority. Only at that point, and not before, would the British government address the issue of self-determination for the population of Palestine. In many Zionist documents, and statements in private, this was a coldly calculated aim: 'No self-determination for the people of Palestine until the people of Palestine have a Jewish majority.' During this period there were a few statesmen who felt that this was unjust. They saw mandates for other countries in operation which were devising and setting up legislative assemblies, initially with veto powers for the mandatory power but with eventual moves towards full independence. But every attempt to do this in Palestine was met with Jewish objections, and the colonial office of the time backed down.

One small example gives the flavour. In 1922 the British colonial office proposed a legislative council of seven Arabs, three Jews and ten representatives nominated by the British. Effectively, any law that discriminated against Arab Palestinians could not be blocked by the Arabs, if the British representatives and the three Jews voted the other way. The Arabs protested. The British changed the makeup to twelve Arabs, eleven British nominees, and three Jews. This was little more than moving deckchairs around on the Titanic. The Arabs could still be outvoted. And even the three Jewish members represented the Jewish community disproportionately. They would have formed 20% of the citizen representatives when Jews were only 10% of the population. It was clear that the British were not sincere in wishing to guide the citizens, the majority of whom were Arabs, towards self-government. The insincerity became clearer when the issue arose of who should vote in elections for any legislative assembly. It was proposed that Arabs get a vote if they could show that they were citizens of Palestine. But many Jews living in Palestine were newly arrived and still retained citizenship of other states. They wanted it that way and didn't want to change from being British or American to being Palestinian. In spite of their pleas to the British for a National Home for world Jews, many of those Jews did not want to commit to leaving the western countries in which they had grown up. So the British first suggested that the qualification for a Jew to vote was that he or she had to promise to apply at *some point* for Palestinian citizenship and to say that when he did that he would renounce any other citizenship he had. This was weaker than the requirement for Arabs, who were required actually to be citizens with Palestinian identity papers. But even dilution of voting qualifications was not enough for the Zionists. They wanted to have their cake and eat it: to promise to apply for citizenship (which was not a commitment at all), but to remain citizens of Britain or America or Germany or wherever they came from. So the British relaxed the rules further to allow dual citizenship – for Jews. But no Arab citizen was allowed to hold more than one nationality. For obvious reasons, the Arabs of Palestine boycotted all such flawed plans for 'representative government'.

It was clear to the Arab Palestinians that the Zionists made all the running in any issue to do with the current and future government of Palestine, and if the Arabs didn't come to terms with that, tough.

Through the 1920s and 1930s, the Palestinian Arabs saw an increase in the immigration of Jews from Europe, accompanied by disproportionate participation of Jews in public life, including major monopolies awarded to Jewish companies without competitive tendering, for electricity supply and other important national utilities. An indication of how statesmanship had flown out of the window by this point was Winston Churchill's argument, as Colonial Secretary, for treating Jewish companies more favourably than Arab companies, and indeed any other foreign companies, in the awarding of large infrastructure projects such as power supply. The biggest scandal in this area, criticised and debated by the few supporters of Palestine in the British parliament, was a major concession given to a Mr Rutenberg, to set up the

Palestine Electric Company with a monopoly of the supply of electricity which made him and his partners a lot of money.

In a debate in parliament, Churchill said:

> Left to themselves, the Arabs of Palestine would not in a thousand years have taken effective steps towards the irrigation and electrification of Palestine. They would have been quite content to dwell – a handful of philosophic people – in the wasted sun-scorched plains, letting the waters of the Jordan continue to flow unbridled and unharnessed into the Dead Sea.

Clearly, by now in the early history of Palestine the main task of Churchill and other government ministers was to say the first thing that came into their heads whether or not it had any basis in fact in order to defend the Zionist project.

Nevertheless, during the early years of the British Mandate there was a touching belief among most Palestinians that the British government was doing its best to ensure a fair and just transition from a society controlled by the Ottomans to an eventual independent Palestine in which the citizens of the state governed themselves. To a certain extent, this belief was encouraged by the British, who knew that it was sensible to give as much time as possible to the preparations for an eventual handover to the Zionists, a handover which they were being pressured to deliver by a powerful lobby in Britain, including a group of M.Ps.

There were occasional objections by ministers and civil servants who saw the injustice inherent in the Balfour Declaration policy, and even official reports including one White Paper, which gave the Arabs hope that perhaps all was not lost. But those hopes were always dashed, on one notorious occasion by the government disowning a balanced White Paper by replacing its recommendations with a pro-Zionist document which the Palestinian Arabs called the Black Letter.

When new plans for a Legislative Council were

abandoned after protests from Zionists who felt it gave the Arabs too much of a say in their own future, a general strike was called among the Palestinian Arabs.

It was the beginning of what became known as the Arab Revolt in Palestine. From 1936 to 1939, there was civil disobedience and outright aggression by Arab bands against the British.

The British army and Palestine police used brutal methods to suppress this violence.

British troops rounded up thousands of Arab villagers and held them in detention camps. By 1939, the total number held reached over 9,000. The British army also carried out search operations on villages suspected of harbouring rebels or hiding weapons.

Men and women would be separated and held in cages, sometimes for days on end. In the village of Halhoul near Hebron in May, 1939, ten men died after being kept in a cage for seven days without food or water. Women were made to bare their breasts to soldiers to prove that they were not rebels in disguise.

Houses were roughly searched, and sometimes food stores were deliberately destroyed by soldiers.

One British citizen wrote in a letter:

> I was ... amazed to see a photograph last night sent home by a British soldier showing an Arab apparently running the gauntlet between two lines of British soldiers who were using big sticks and the butts of rifles... The soldier who sent it had written on the back 'This is how we made the "Wog" talk. Wouldn't the Berlin boys make a shout about this if they saw it?' One British soldier has his stick up in the air and the Arab is jumping to escape the blow.[3]

---

[3] CO 733/371/2

Another, resident in Palestine, wrote in a letter:

> Parties of troops move along street by street and house by house. Each house as they reach it is cleared of its male inhabitants, who are passed by military patrols to a large collecting centre usually located in an open square or space. Here the inhabitants are required to squat or sit on the pavement. A little drill is at this stage frequently imparted. The troops explain through an interpreter that any man standing up without a previous command to do so will be shot. The command is then given in English 'Up' – then 'Down' – Up, Down, and then a quicker tempo 'Up-Down-Up-Down'. Anyone not quick enough gets a kick up the backside. Due subjection having been thus established en masse, the male populace is interrogated man by man. 'Where do you live? What is your work?' etc. This goes on till dusk, when the balance still uninterrogated are marched off to a prison camp until the morning.[4]

The Arab Revolt was eventually called off, after an appeal by leaders of other Arab states, but in any case it was clear to the Palestinian Arabs that the British were determined to deal harshly with any Arab attempts to resist the gradual handover of their country to Jews. In the course of their suppression of the Arab protest movement, the British effectively deprived the Arabs of the people and methods which might have helped them resist more strongly the assaults of the Zionists when they eventually came in 1947-8.

It was interesting to see how, in the following years, Jewish terrorism in Palestine was dealt with far more leniently by the authorities. Collective punishment of the sort used on innocent Arab villagers was rarely attempted against the residents of well-armed Jewish settlements who harboured Jewish

---

[4] Quoted in O.S. Edwardes, *Palestine: Land of Broken Promises*, Dorothy Crisp & Co, 1946, p. 110

terrorists and even praised their actions. On the occasions when police or soldiers tried to enter in pursuit of terrorists or in search of arms, they were met by kibbutz residents with sticks and sometimes guns, and often turned back.

The last nine years of the British Mandate unfolded in parallel with World War II. Not only were the British government's attention and resources needed elsewhere – depriving Palestine of any serious governmental consideration of its future – but a new factor gained increasing importance in the case made by Zionists for Palestine to be made a Jewish state. The world became increasingly aware of the Nazi persecution of the Jews and of the horrors of concentration camps. Political Zionists in Europe and the USA used this appalling persecution to reinforce their arguments that Palestine should be a Jewish state, a haven for those Jews who might survive or escape the persecution.

There are three things wrong with this argument.

First, although this plea was spread far and wide on behalf of the Jews, there was no evidence that the majority of the worst persecuted Jews wanted to go and live in a small Middle Eastern country with which they felt no connection. In fact, many of them desperately wanted to go to countries with the same Judaeo-Christian values and culture of the countries from which they came. This meant Britain, Europe, the US, Canada, even South America. Instead, the political Zionist movement painted a picture of Palestine as the only salvation for these distressed Jews of Europe.

Second, the movement to take over Palestine for the Jews concealed or downplayed the fact that Palestine was an Arab country, with a minority population of Jews, most of them recent immigrants. Even by 1946, the Arabs were still in the majority.

Third, there was no mention of the fact that the Palestinians had nothing to do with the persecution of the Jews in Europe and yet, if the Jewish state was achieved, they would be punished by the loss of their country and their freedom.

As with the Balfour Declaration, one party – the Zionist movement – was asking another party – the first world nations

41

– to give away the land of a third party – the Palestinians – who had no say in the matter.

At the same time as international pressure on the British government was being whipped up, most notably by American Jews, to accelerate immigration in order to give Palestine a Jewish majority, there was a different sort of pressure in Palestine which made it more and more difficult for Britain to govern Palestine and in particular to protect the rights of the indigenous Palestinian Arabs.

While British policy in the 20s and 30s had been to bend over backwards to give Jewish Palestinians more rights than was justified by the proportion of the population they formed, this wasn't enough for many Jews in Palestine who wanted a Jewish state to be set up immediately in Palestine.

As a result, and stung into action by the intensifying persecution of Jews in German-controlled Europe, a campaign of Jewish terror was initiated against British police, soldiers and civilians, and against Palestinian Arabs. At the height of the terror, restaurant and cinema massacres, car bombs, bombs in markets, and attacks on police, were almost a daily occurrence, at a rate and intensity which was not seen again until ISIS did its worst in the 21st century Middle East.

These attacks were carried out by two Jewish gangs, the Stern gang and the Irgun, often supported by Haganah which was the 'official' Jewish militia, allowed by the British to defend Jews in Palestine.

The terrorists even attacked their own people, killing Jews who did not support terror morally or financially.

In a fund-raising advertisement in the *New York Times*, headed *Letter to Terrorists*, the writer Ben Hecht wrote:

> Every time you blow up a British arsenal, or wreck a British jail, or send a British railroad train sky high, or rob a British bank, or let go with your guns and bombs at the British betrayers and invaders of your homeland, the Jews of America make a little holiday in their hearts.

These appeals were very successful. Between 1939 and

1948, the Jewish Agency raised 344 million dollars, about two and a half billion pounds in today's money, enough to fund many illegal immigration ships, and illegal arms caches.

An idea of the 'justification' offered for these atrocities comes in a Stern Gang pamphlet found in Haifa:

> The British blood-sucker, be he a soldier, a constable, a clerk, so long as he obeys orders to exploit and murder, he is indicted. He is here to guard the imperialist rule and prevent the rescue of the Jews. For this his blood will be shed. ... Let those among us who are afraid of bloodshed and destruction say openly that they surrender to a New Munich, to each White Paper, which leads to a ghetto and ultimately to new gas-chambers a la Auschwitz. ... They cry over defiled British blood, but remain silent over the blood of innocent refugees .... Jewish blood is sacred and pure. The blood of Britons suppressing foreign countries is defiled. Therefore it will be shed to prevent innocent blood from being shed.[5]

The tone of this and other pamphlets issued by Jewish terrorist groups during the 1940s has uncomfortable overtones of today's ISIS propaganda statements issued after its atrocities. The statements are not overtly religious and try to echo the resistance of indigenous peoples to imperialism. But the "sacredness" of Jewish blood is a pseudo-religious concept. And of course the true indigenous people are the Palestinian Arabs, and the true imperialists are those European and American Jews who wanted to take over their country.

Although this pamphlet raises the spectre of 'new gas-chambers' it was issued two years after the end of World War II, when Germany and the Nazis had been soundly defeated. But the Zionists, with no legal basis for claiming

---

[5] Document from file War Office 275/109, Public Record Office, London.

that Palestine should be a Jewish state, needed to keep the flame of anti-semitism alive. A cartoon in a British newspaper by a leading political cartoonist, David Low, shows a British soldier standing in a road in Palestine and behind him are two Jewish terrorists ready to set off a bomb. One terrorist is saying to the other "What, he's not anti-semitic? We'll soon alter that."

As the 1940s unfolded, Palestine became embedded in two parallel universes. There was the universe of Whitehall, parliament, government ministries, defence budgets and growing public outrage mainly at British deaths (although hundreds of Arabs were being killed too). Here, Palestine was mainly a news topic, like the economy, the Cold War, the Groundnut Scheme, or the Marshall Plan.

In the Middle East, Palestine was a country, with large towns and small villages, people trying to make a living, agriculture, a multi-layered society of middle class and working class people, and a Palestinian nationalism that was growing alongside Arab nationalism. In one universe, it didn't really matter what happened to Palestine and its inhabitants, unless it affected British expenditure and resources, or generated unpleasant publicity for the government. In the other, there was a growing realisation that the country in which most Arab citizens had roots stretching back generations was in danger of being handed over to an alien group, and the Palestinians were not going to be consulted about it.

There are parallels with Iraq today. In Britain, it is an irritant, because of its regular violence – at least no longer affecting British troops – and because of the realisation that the wrong decisions were made early on in the post-war life of the country and then no decisions were made when governments became paralysed by the unforeseen consequences of those wrong decisions.

The British and Americans backed one horse over the other in a two-horse race – just as in Palestine – and now have to live with the consequences. Or rather they don't because the consequences – as with Palestine – are taking place thousands of miles from Whitehall and the White House and principally affecting the inhabitants of the blighted country.

This 'two universe' situation was exploited to the hilt by the Zionists up to and beyond 1948, when Britain washed its hands of Palestine.

The UN General Assembly was asked to vote on a plan drawn up by a UN committee which suggested dividing the territory of Palestine into two states – a Jewish state and an Arab one. This sounds quite even-handed until you put it another way – the plan suggested taking away more than half of the area of Palestine, still a country with an Arab majority, and handing it over to the Jews of the world. What's more, the area allocated for a Jewish state would still have a population that was 45% Arab.

What the UN decided was perhaps the most bitter pill for Palestinians to swallow. The UN debate could have been a turning point for the Palestinians. After facing decades of their rights being denied, here was a new international body set up to promote peace and justice in the world. Surely, the UN would come up with a just solution.

When the UN discussed the partition plan, there were plenty of delegates who thought dividing up the land would be a gross injustice to the Arabs.

In fact, there was a point in the debate where it looked as if the partition resolution would not obtain the necessary majority. As the Zionists and their American supporters totted up the numbers it was clear they might lose unless some countries chose to change their views – or were compelled to.

What happened next was described by the Liberian delegate in an anguished conversation with an American diplomat, who reported the conversation in a secret memo. The Liberian complained that, although Liberia was against partition he'd received a warning that if he didn't vote for partition, Liberia could expect "no further favours" from the US Congress.

The pressure worked, as Harold Beeley, a British diplomatic observer at the vote, reported to the Foreign Office. He described the countries that had changed their votes as "repentant sinners" and said that their "embarrassment

... was increased by the rapturous welcome each received from the New York press." [6]

> Particularly ludicrous was the position of the Philippine and Haitian delegates who were obliged to vote in favour of partition three days after they had spoken against it.

There is of course something familiar-sounding about these events – America issuing threats to UN members to make them vote for a manifestly unjust decision in the Israel/Palestine conflict. At least with US threats in 2017 designed to get support for moving its embassy to Jerusalem, the pressure failed. Unfortunately, with the partition vote the threats succeeded, and when the votes were counted, three delegates who had spoken out strongly *against* partition, nevertheless voted for it and the die was cast.

Someone asked President Harry S. Truman why he had put so much weight behind the Zionist claim on Palestine, and he said:

> I am sorry but I have to answer to hundreds of thousands who are anxious for the success of Zionism. I do not have hundreds of thousands of Arabs among my constituents.

By the terms of the partition plan, more than half of Palestine was to become a Jewish state, with the remnant as an Arab state. But the so-called Jewish state would still have a large Arab population, 45% of the total. Overnight, some people who had lived in the portion of the Arab state of Palestine handed to the Jews were told that they were now citizens of a Jewish state. With the disappearance of British control – which had at least a semblance of respect for the rights of all citizens – the Arab population were now at the mercy of a group who had plotted for thirty years to take over the

---

[6] F.O. 371/68528

land and had now succeeded. "At the mercy" sounds a strong phrase. After all, there were times in those thirty years where some Zionist leaders said, at least in public, that they were willing to share the state with its existing population and bring them the benefits of Jewish expertise, resources and financial management. In fact, as copious diary entries, confidential correspondence and internal Zionist communications later revealed, the true aim of the Zionists was an exclusively Jewish state with few or no Arabs living in it.

This then was the first pillar of injustice – the creation among people who didn't think or know much about the Middle East of the idea that Palestine should be, by right, a Jewish state.

The second pillar of injustice was the actions taken by the Zionists, and eventually the Israelis as they became, to turn the idea of Palestine as a Jewish state into facts on the ground. This presented the new state with a problem. It was actually one they had started to solve in 1947 when it became clear that the British would leave and that some kind of division of Palestine would occur. The problem was that the supporters and proponents of the new state wanted it to be exclusively Jewish, with no Arabs remaining.

Menachem Begin, terrorist leader and future prime minister of Israel, said after the UN vote:

> The partition of the Homeland is illegal. It will never be recognized. …It will not bind the Jewish people. Jerusalem was and will forever be our capital. Eretz Israel (the land of Israel) will be restored to the people of Israel. All of it. And forever.

Such sentiments among the Jewish leaders led to the notorious Plan Dalet, denied at the time but revealed in all its horrors in later years.

Plan Dalet was a military plan to ensure that as few as possible of the Arab Palestinians remained in the Jewish state after its foundation.

The level and intensity of the planning to achieve a Jewish Palestine is clear from the fact that this was the fourth plan devised to suppress Palestinian resistance to the takeover of their state and that the first was laid in 1945, when there was no clear end to the British mandate.

Plans Aleph, Bet, Gimel and Dalet, the first letters of the Hebrew alphabet, were a successive escalation of a military campaign to take Palestine. When this campaign was mentioned in public at all, it was presented as entirely defensive. But defending the potential new state against whom? To admit publicly that it was a campaign to attack, expel or massacre the indigenous inhabitants of the land, people who, under the UN vote, were meant to be protected, might be a step too far even for the increasingly self-righteous Zionist propagandists. Instead, then and ever since, Plans Aleph to Dalet have been presented as a reluctant response by the Jewish forces to the hostility of Palestinians, supported by Arab states, to the outpouring of world support for a Jewish state, but the truth is precisely the opposite.

The UN vote for partition was the response of the world community to decades of pressure, threats, and terrorism which led to Britain abandoning the mandate and handing the problem over to the UN. The Palestinians – perhaps to their own disadvantage – were remarkably restrained in the face of increasing provocation. This restraint was commented on time and again in official British communications from the Palestine government to Whitehall. Much good did it do them. When push came to shove – and what a shove – the Palestinians were powerless to resist the combined military forces, resources and propaganda of the Zionist movement which was determined to make Palestine an exclusively Jewish state.

There was participation of forces from other Arab countries but this was not an unalloyed blessing for the indigenous Palestinians. These were no match for a well-supplied and long-planned Jewish military campaign. But their role has been deliberately distorted in an attempt to make a *casus belli* for Jewish action. Even today, the story of "Arab forces massing to push the Jews into the sea" is regularly trotted out in print and at meetings. Most ordinary Jews with no special interest in the topic still believe this propaganda myth. One can understand why. It is more comforting than to believe the truth – which they have probably never heard anyway – that there was a campaign of ethnic cleansing, planned from 1945 and carried out through 1947 and 1948, to get rid of as many Palestinians as possible, so that Israel could be a racially-defined state, as far as possible *"Arabrein"* – Arab free – to twist a German word used by the Nazis.

In fact, as is clear from archival evidence, the intention of the forces from Arab countries was to protect the areas allocated to the Palestinian Arabs by the UN Partition Plan from invasion by the Jewish armies, not to invade the Jewish areas. They are often described as 'invading' Palestine. Indeed they did, but Palestine was full of Palestinians, Arabs like the soldiers of the Arab armies – why should they not? But there can have been no gentler 'invasion' than this crossing of the border from Trans-Jordan to protect the people on the other side of the border from those who wanted to steal their land. And when Israel and its supporters talk about the Arab armies invading 'Palestine' they want people to believe that the armies were actually invading Israel, which they did not do.

That the Palestinians needed the protection of the Arab armies – which in fact they failed to provide – is clear both from Plan Dalet and from what actually happened. Plan Dalet was drawn up to expand Jewish-held areas beyond those allocated to the proposed Jewish State in the UN Partition Plan. In other words, to steal even more of Arab Palestine than had been allocated by the UN. There is no ambiguity about this aim or about the methods – to destroy Arab villages on both sides of the border and expel or kill the inhabitants on the grounds of their ethnicity. To make the task easier for the soldiers, who might occasionally have hesitated to kill innocent villagers, Arab villages were defined as "enemy bases." By definition, then, anyone who was found in a village – an enemy base – is an enemy and can be destroyed or sent into exile.

Methodically, the Alphabet Plans were executed village by village, along with many Palestinians, in areas the Jews had coveted for decades. It didn't take long for news of the Jewish ethnic cleansing campaign to spread from village to village and town to town. Many Palestinian families were connected by marriage across the towns and villages of Palestine. You would need a lot of courage, on learning of the death or expulsion of relatives and friends by the Jewish militias, to carry on with normal life. The deliberate spread by Jewish forces of atrocity stories and of rumours was a useful instrument to get people to leave their homes.

Entire villages were cleared in this way and many of them destroyed. Although many Palestinians left temporarily, as they saw it, to return after the hostilities were over, there were often no homes to return to and, in any case, the new Jewish state refused to admit anyone who was ethnically Arab, whatever his or her long-term connection with Palestine.

After completing the ethnic cleansing of Palestine, the systematic destruction of the Palestinian landscape began. First, a wave of plunder and looting of Arab homes and businesses took place by Jews from nearby Jewish settlements and by Israeli soldiers. Villages and parts of towns were destroyed to obliterate the traces of Palestinian presence and to prevent the return of the refugees to their homes.

After 1948, a wave of destruction, organised by the Israeli army, the public works authorities, the Jewish Agency and the Jewish National Fund, had the purpose of removing all trace, both past and present, of Palestinians from the state. The project was helped by Jewish archaeologists, who wanted to ensure that only Palestinian history was destroyed, not the more sparse evidence of Jewish presence in the land.

When the dust settled, and the new state of Israel took its place on the world stage, its founding myths swallowed wholesale by the nations which rushed to recognise it, the original inhabitants of Palestine found themselves in different locations in the world, deprived of even the minimal rights they had held as citizens of a territory under the British Mandate.

Now we come to the third pillar of injustice. In 1948 the new state of Israel was still in only part of the ancient land of Palestine. Zionism had always coveted the entire land between the Jordan and the Mediterranean and had ended up with 'only'

78% of it. (Hardly anyone these days remembers that Israel was allocated 55% under the Partition plan and stole another 23% by its campaign of expulsion, destruction and occupation in 1947-9.) There is no doubt that Israel's long term aim was and is to take the remaining 22%. Privately, its political and military leaders said so firmly and regularly. So the succession of wars between 1956 and the present day are part of an overall plan to fulfil that aim, through a series of contrived excuses to attack its neighbours on various pretexts.

This story is full of oddities and inconsistencies in Israel's case which have gone unnoticed. Take the Six Day War in 1967. Israel's manufactured excuse was that it was under threat of extermination from Egypt. (It wasn't.) But its covert ultimate war aim was directed against the Palestinians living in the West Bank and Gaza. Even if the Egyptians *had* posed a threat, the Palestinians certainly didn't. Nevertheless, they became again 'the victims of the victims', just as had happened after World War II.

Israel's actions since 1948 have been a continuation of its war against the Palestinians, most notably the occupation of land Israel has always coveted, in Syria, on the West Bank and in Gaza. As a result, and because of what is clearly an illegal act under international law, the focus of Palestinian diplomatic activity has been to regain at least the land which was occupied by Israel in 1967, only part of the areas allocated to the Arabs under the UN partition resolution. For many people, and some nations, the idea has got around that if only Israel would hand back the territories it took in 1967, the conflict will be solved. Such people, and such nations, have clearly never talked to – or at least listened to – Palestinians.

The conflict will never be solved until the root cause is addressed – dispossession of the entire land of Palestine. This can only happen if Palestinians are given the right to return to a Palestine in which all their national, religious and political rights are respected.

But it is not just the loss of land and rights that is the cause of continuing Palestinian hostility. It is the way Israel and many Jews throughout the world have failed to admit that this dispossession took place at all or that it was deliberate, illegal and inhuman. To add insult to injury, the Palestinians are even blamed for their own misfortune: "they chose to leave", as if there wasn't a well-organised plan to get rid of as many Palestinians as possible from the Jewish state. Indeed, a major grievance for the new state of Israel is that although they had expelled three quarters of a million Palestinians, there were still Palestinian Arabs who remained, because their villages were not part of the ethnic cleansing campaign, or because they lived in larger towns, some with mixed Jewish and Arab communities. But there were also towns, like my family's ancestral home of Safad, where the entire Arab community of 10,000 was 'cleansed' while the 1,500 Jewish inhabitants remained behind, and more Jewish families took over Arab houses, property and valuables.

So the continuing hostility today of Palestinians to Israel is a potent and enduring mix of loss, suffering, neglect of rights, ineradicable memory and outrage at Israeli lies about the true origins of the conflict. The Occupation and settlements on Arab land play only a part. No diaspora Jew who claims a right to live in Israel has the same connection with the land as any Palestinian. Most Jewish immigrants, from the 1920s and 1930s until today, have ancestors who can show no demonstrable link with the land other than a sentimental, religiously-inspired attachment to a part of the globe they have been told stories about. Most Palestinians can name the precise place in Palestine where their parents, grandparents and great-grandparents came from, and continue to keep alive a desire to reactivate that connection. That is why they have to be offered the right to return before this conflict which has gone on far too long can be solved.

The next chapter will present a picture of the different groups of Palestinians, where they are in the world, and their differing social characteristics. This will lead in turn into a consideration of how those groups might respond to the establishment of a genuine right of return as part of an overall peace settlement based on the recreation of Palestine and Israel as a single democratic state.

3 The Palestinians

I n 2007 I was visiting the Sabra and Shatila Palestinian refugee camps in Lebanon. These camps are notorious because they were the scene of a massacre perpetrated by right wing Lebanese militias with the consent and protection of the Israel Defence Forces and its leader Ariel Sharon who were meant to be in control of the camps at the time. These massacres were a reminder of how the Palestinians have turned into the victims of the victims. It is as if the European Jews, persecuted by the Nazis in an attempt to exterminate them, have ever since felt the need to take their anger and bitterness on people they *could* rather than on people they should.

The Palestinians did nothing wrong in seeking to remain in their homes in the country they had lived in for generations, but that is exactly what they have been punished for, ever since 1948. It is true that as Israel remained intransigent and self-righteous, and continued to persecute even the Palestinians who remained in Israel, a resistance movement, the PLO, was formed which used violence to draw attention to the issue of Palestinian rights that the world had ignored since 1948. In a cycle that has continued to the present day, Israeli actions lead to Palestinian resistance which are then painted as the initiating factor for further Israeli violence. "We had to defend ourselves," the Israelis say, rather as the Nazis might have said when they burned 642 people to death in a church in Oradour because an SS officer had been captured by the French resistance.

There are at least 12 million Palestinians in the world today, descended from the original inhabitants of Mandate Palestine, about one and a quarter million, 750,000 of whom were expelled in 1948. (Those who remained were divided between the West Bank and Gaza, and the new state of Israel.) There are estimated to be 30-50,000 refugees still alive from that initial exodus. The Palestinians in the refugee camps are one of three roughly distinct groups of Palestinians around the world today. In this chapter I will describe each group and how they came to be where they are. These distinctions will be relevant later in the book to the issue of how the right of return will need to be operated in different ways depending on the choices made by Palestinians and how these choices are likely to differ depending on which group a Palestinian belongs to.

It's worth saying something about the reasons the refugees left, because the exodus triggered some useful myths spread by the Israelis which have served to paint the Palestinians as the cause of their own dispossession. Clearly, if at the time Israel and its army had been revealed as planning and executing a mass expulsion of Palestinians, what has since been called ethnic cleansing, they might have lost the sympathy of the world, which at the time had been persuaded that the only reason for the establishment of Israel was as a haven for survivors from the holocaust in Europe. So, to conceal the truth, Israel maintained, and still tries to maintain, that the Palestinians left of their own free will, and perhaps were even persuaded by their own leaders to leave, with the understanding that they would return soon when the victorious Arab armies had pushed the Jews into the sea. None of this is true, of course, but it serves to deflect attention from what really went on. However, one interesting thing about this story is that it implies that had the Palestinians not left Israel they would still be living in their homes, admittedly under Jewish rule but still far better off than the new life that followed their flight.

Two things give the lie to that idea. First, the efforts made by Israel after 1948 to expel or make life difficult for those Palestinians who were slow to leave the country or tried to turn back before they reached the borders. The second is the unrelenting discrimination against those Palestinian Arabs who did stay in Israel, obviously in an attempt to make their lives as difficult as possible in the hope that they might leave. That discrimination was at its worst in the years up to 1956, a period when the Arab citizens of Israel were placed under military rule and their rights curtailed in all sort of ways, analogous to the pass laws then operating for the blacks in South Africa. Far from wishing the Palestinians had stayed, Israel from its inception made clear its wish that the state had as few Palestinians in it as possible, and did its best to achieve this. Even since military rule was lifted in Israel itself, Palestinians have been discriminated against at every level of state control, from national government down to municipal administration. Israel bristles at the term 'apartheid' but the evidence for racist discrimination against Israeli Arabs at an official level is too strong to deny, and once you start looking at informal attitudes to Arabs among Jewish Israelis, you find rampant racism which you could call 'the new antisemitism' since Arabs are semites too. An Israeli Jewish friend of mine who, unusually, has many Arab friends, was asked by a Jewish friend "Have you ever seen an Arab hug his children?" It is difficult to understand such a weird question and guess at where it came from. I can only suggest that it might have something to do with the image promoted by successive right wing governments that all Palestinians are terrorists who send their children out to be suicide bombers and therefore clearly don't show the parental feelings of normal people.

No Palestinian chose to be a refugee. Even those who left by choice believed that Israel would respect the normal rules of war and allow them back after hostilities ceased.

Of course, we now know that Israel respects no norms of international behaviour. It has been criticised over 90 times in the UN Security Council for violations of U.N. Security Council resolutions, the U.N. Charter, the Geneva Conventions, international terrorism law, or other violations of international law and just ignores such criticisms with contempt.

I see the refugees in camps as being the most unfortunate of all the groups, and most deserving of efforts to be made even 70 years after their dispossession to redress in some way the losses they have suffered, both material and psychological.

It is easy to infer from the current situation of many of these Palestinians that somehow they were always poor, deprived, living in cramped surroundings and often unemployed, surviving on aid from UNWRA, the UN organisation set up after 1948 to deal with the huge efflux from Israel. Although no longer living in tents, the refugees in Sabra and Shatila live in slum housing created hastily with poor construction, inadequate utilities, minimal lighting and variable power supplies. Without wishing to make them sound like noble savages, there is a dignity in the average Palestinian camp residence, with the refugees making the best of a very bad job, as people sleep and eat in circumstances which are far from the social environment in Palestine from which many of their parents and grandparents came.

The social status of the people who were expelled from Palestine in 1947-8 covered all professions, occupations and income levels. Those who were not lucky enough to find transport out of Palestine to Lebanon, Gaza, Jordan or Egypt, were forced to walk, often leaving all their possessions behind. One of my cousins, a young woman at the time from a good family, walked from Safad in northern Palestine to Damascus, about 80 km, and her shoes were in shreds when she arrived. The populations of whole towns, like Ramleh and Lydda, were expelled and force-marched without food or water to the border and then left to fend for themselves. As the magnitude of the expulsions became apparent, hasty camps were set up in territories all round the borders of the new state of Israel, and people of differing backgrounds thrown together. But what they had in common was an attachment to the places they had left, and that attachment, based on facts passed down the generations, has never left most Palestinians. In the camps, it manifests itself in a touching and unusual way. First, because the expelled Palestinians took the shortest route to territories outside Israel, the locations of the camps represent broadly a projection across the border of the places in Palestine from which the inhabitants come. So the camps in southern Lebanon harbour people who left northern Palestine, notably the Galilee area. The camps in Gaza are a reflection of towns and villages in southern Palestine, and the camps in the West Bank are home to people from towns and villages in the middle of Palestine.

And because people in the camps came from the same area of Palestine, there is a further way in which the geography of Palestine is mirrored, in the layout of the streets and alleys. Often the refugees from one area will live in the same street or group of apartments in the camp, and nearby will be families from adjacent villages in Palestine. Just as marriages took place in Palestine between families who lived near each other, often repeating a pattern which had started several generations ago, the same happens in the camps.

This reflects a psychological and emotional connection not only with the country of Palestine, but with specific towns and villages, and even with houses, which the current generation has never seen. Reinforced by photo albums and family trees, the connection of most, if not all, Palestinians with Palestine is as strong today as it was for their parents and grandparents seventy years ago, confounding the hope expressed by many of the founders of Israel that "the Palestinians will soon give up and get on with their lives." That huge misjudgement has bedevilled Israel's attempts since its founding, using oppression, violence and entry bans, to make Palestinians give up their claim to the land.

This is relevant to the issue of the right of return. I believe that the geographical attachment to Palestine, shown in the layouts of some refugee camps, is just an intensification of a feeling that many Palestinians have, including those who are better off than those defined officially as refugees and more assimilated in other countries. It could be argued – as some Jews do – that this attachment to Palestine is just kept alive in order to prolong the conflict. It is suggested that Palestinians in other Arab countries are deliberately kept in the status of refugees when they could become obedient Lebanese, Syrians, Jordanians, Kuwaitis, Emiratis or Egyptians. This is what Israel would like, of course. If Palestinians were assimilated into their host countries, Palestine might become a distant folk memory and no longer be retained as a place to which Palestinians would ultimately return. But that isn't going to happen. In the three groups I shall deal with, I would put Palestinians in refugee camps in the group most likely to take up an offer to return to Palestine, when that offer is made. (Those who turn down the offer, as I suggest later, will have other options which recognise what they have suffered and lost.) There are just over a million and a half refugees in camps around the Middle East.

The second group of refugees, better off than the Palestinians in camps, are those who also remained in the Middle East, making homes and careers for themselves in other Arab countries. Most of my own close relatives came into this group, settling in Lebanon or Jordan or Egypt or the West Bank. Their route out of Palestine was similar to the camp refugees, a disorganised flight triggered by news or rumours of Jewish threats and atrocities. My relatives came from the north and many of them travelled by boat or lorry or even on foot to Beirut or Damascus. They were largely middle class people and could afford to pay for transport wherever it could be found, leaving behind homes, property, and valuables with the intention of returning once the fighting had stopped and some semblance of sanity returned to the country. Of course, they never did, excluded by the new Israeli government, who handed over their homes, lands and property to recent Jewish immigrants from Europe. Many such refugees had family or social connections with other Arab countries which eased the problems of being forced to abandon Palestine overnight. Like the refugees in camps, they are reminded daily of their loss by their proximity to Israel. In the occupied territories these reminders are starkest since they take the form of Israeli soldiers, checkpoints, and settlers, associated with people who can drive in fifteen minutes to the lost towns and villages of Palestine which are barred to Palestinians who live a few miles away. I have a relative by marriage who was born and brought up in Jerusalem and has not been there – officially – for decades because she would be turned back at the checkpoint. She is like someone born in Oxford who lives in Woodstock and can never return to her birthplace. At least this second group has been able to make or remake lives for themselves, sometimes lives of some prosperity, and of course, this provides the time and the resources to form the core of Palestinian activism. Even Palestinians in this second group who went further afield but stayed in the Middle East have helped to keep alive a spirit – known as 'sumud' or steadfastness – which has successfully kept the Palestinian narrative in front of the world, aided of course by Israel's heavy-handed, and in the end counterproductive, attempts to deny the justice of the Palestinian cause. One member of this group was Yasser Arafat, an engineer by training who worked in Kuwait and Egypt and gathered around him a movement, the PLO, which did more than any other to keep Palestine in the forefront of world affairs.

The Arab world Palestinians, if I can call them that, will have a range of attitudes to the possibility of return. If they are in the West Bank and Gaza, at least a Gaza which is reconstructed and habitable again, they may wish to stay where they are, particularly if they are not far geographically from their original homes. But a refugee who lives near Hebron and came from the Galilee is likely to want to return to his ancestral town or village. If they live in Jordan, say, where a large number of Palestinians live, perhaps 70% of the total population, I'm sure a large number would seek to return to Palestine, something which would make a major difference to the nature of Jordan as a state. On the other hand, those who chose to remain would receive compensation which would help the Jordanian economy. Indeed, there is also an argument that the 'host nations' who received Palestinian refugees in 1948 and 1967 would benefit directly from compensation for the costs incurred.

The third group is those Palestinians who left the Arab world and set up new lives far away from their ancestral land. My father was in that group, not by intention but because when the time came when he might have returned to Palestine, the land had become Israel and like all Palestinians abroad he was banned. (The only time he did return, much later in his life, was when he travelled secretly in 1975 with Henry Kissinger from Syria to Israel in Air Force One, and while Kissinger was on official business my father spent some time with his sister whom he hadn't seen since the 1940s. But that's another story.) This group is likely to have a different attitude again to the right of return. But before exploring their possible options, I need to emphasise one thing: no Palestinian, wherever he or she is, will ever give up a belief that they are entitled to that right. To do so would suggest that in some sense, a Palestinian believed that Israel was justified in taking away Palestinian land and expelling or barring its rightful inhabitants. It is up to any Palestinian to choose not to return, but then he or she would still expect compensation for losses and distress.

Many from among the third group of Palestinians I have spoken to have personal conflicts over the right of return as applied to their own situations. To some extent this applies to me and my family so maybe it is best if I try to express that conflict.

Even if a Palestinian, usually of the younger generation, has never visited his ancestral home, there is a strong family awareness of the details of that place, down to the house and even the rooms in the house where a parent or grandparent grew up. There is a rich layered narrative which he or she will have imbibed, and of which there will often be reminders in photo albums, maps, embroideries or pictures on the wall, mementoes such as keys or coffee sets, and even a circle of friends and relatives, also in exile, with whom regular contact will involve retelling of stories of "the old days" or even new family links derived in some sense from the fact that family A used to live in this village and family B used to live in that village five miles away on the other side of a hill in Galilee.

Whatever their attitude to the possibility of a permanent return to Palestine, selling up in London or New York, say, and moving into a house in or near to the previous family home, the third group of Palestinians is likely to value the opportunity of reinforcing the link with Palestine in some way. At the moment, those of us well off enough to visit Palestine get a lot of pleasure and reinforcement of identity by visiting parts of Israel that retain the character and sometimes the demography of pre-1948 Palestine. The city of Jaffa, for example, of which Tel Aviv was once a dusty satellite village, although much ravaged, destroyed and overlaid, is still an Arab city with a proud history and residents who include some old Palestinian families 'clinging to the wreckage'. In Chapter 9 I suggest a way in the affinity with Palestine which many Palestinians feel even if they have rarely or ever been there can be incorporated into a right of return programme in a way which is cost effective and recognises their desire to stay where they are but have a permanent link with the land of their ancestors.

4   Blind alleys

One thing needs to be said at the outset. From its establishment, Israel has had no genuine interest in a 'solution' to its dispute with Palestinians. Its aim from May 15th 1948 has been to do everything it could to acquire more territory than it was allocated under the UN Partition Plan, and to expel or otherwise remove all the former inhabitants of the land from within its boundaries.

Zionist literature, written and agreed with, often in secret, by people who became the political and military leaders in Palestine, was unambiguous about the desire – indeed it was seen as a right – for the whole area between the river Jordan and the Mediterranean Sea to become an exclusively Jewish state. Any statements to the contrary, allowing perhaps, for some Arab Palestinians to live in the area, were purely for public consumption. This is still the situation. There may be individual Israelis – a small number – who accept that, of course, those Palestinians who live now in Palestine have an absolute right to live there rather than being intruders. A slightly larger number, perhaps, accept that for practical reasons – the achievement of stability and security, or even just to avoid being an international pariah – Israel should agree to share the land fairly with its previous inhabitants. But few members, if any, of these two groups have ever achieved political power in Israel, and certainly today Israeli politicians are more obdurate than they have ever been about maintaining an exclusively Jewish state and presenting – at least to the Israeli electorate – plans for the elimination of Palestinians from any political or civil participation in the land that was once theirs.

This chapter will not set out in detail the various plans that have been proposed, usually by powers far away from the scene of the conflict. There are numerous books that attempt that sterile task. Madrid, Geneva, Oslo, Camp David, Sharm-el-Sheikh – there is a roll-call of locations where politicians have stayed in luxury hotels, their bags crammed with maps and schemes, and worked away at the task of trying to square the circle to Jewish-Palestinian accord. Well, I say "worked away at the task" but that applied only to the Arabs and the Western powers who instigated the talks in each case. I believe that the Israelis in these discussions had no interest in any genuine solution, other than one that would give them everything they wanted, and give the Palestinian Arabs nothing. Enough inside accounts of these negotiations have emerged to show (a) the incompetence of Arab negotiators in the face of Israel's overwhelming political, statistical, demographic, and cartographical expertise, and (b) the desire of the facilitating major powers to get *any* solution at all rather than a fair and just one.

All the so-called 'peace talks' have been based on one Israeli premise – give the Arabs the minimum and take the maximum. Of course, history shows that Israel has always wanted to take rather than give. The ideal solution for Israel would be for the Palestinians to go away somewhere else so that Jews could have a state stretching from the Jordan to the Mediterranean. So each set of plans for a solution has had that implicit premise.

They can all be characterised as 'two-state' solutions, with an Israel and a Palestine living side by side in mutual dislike.

Not since UN mediator Count Folke Bernadotte has there been any serious proposal for some kind of federation of the two peoples, with economic, social and civil collaboration. (Count Bernadotte, by the way, was assassinated by a future Prime Minister of Israel, Yitzhak Shamir, who was amnestied by the new state of Israel for his crime almost as soon as he had committed it.)

There are two key 'tricks' which Israel has used in all these discussions. One is to take its starting point for parcelling out the land as the temporary borders existing after the armistice between Israel and the Arabs in 1949, when in fact, by that date it had stolen a significant amount more land before the armistice was signed.

The second 'trick' has been to use the word 'compromise' in ways which defy logic and semantics.

This is how it works:

In 1947, the UN General Assembly voted, after much lobbying, bribery and threats, to divide Palestine into two separate states. (By the way, General Assembly votes were not binding on anyone, in the way that Security Council resolutions are, but the UN was in its infancy and nothing like the Palestine issue had ever occurred in its short life.) The Jewish state was to have 55% of the territory and Palestine was to have 45%. This was in a situation where the larger portion, that given to the Jews, contained 538,000 Jews, and the smaller portion contained

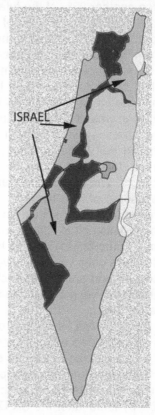

ISRAEL

804,000 Arabs. There were also 397,000 Arabs whose homes were in the Jewish area and would be expected to live in the new Jewish state. In fact, from before the declaration of independence in 1948, Jewish forces had started trying to acquire land that had been allocated to the Palestinian Arabs in the Partition Plan, and even to expel Arabs from their villages in those areas. This continued after May 1948 when Israel declared independence. As a result of the Israeli army entering the Arab areas and taking over Palestinian land, in spite of efforts by Arab armies to prevent them (not to "push them into the sea" but to stop the encroachment), by the time an armistice was signed in 1949, Israel had taken by force another 23% of the total area of Palestine. This meant that Israel now had 78% of pre-1948 Palestine instead of the allocated 55%, leaving the Arabs with 22% of the land in which they had originally been the great majority.

So at a stroke, the Palestinians had lost to the Jews nearly a half of the land that they had been allocated by the UN. The map on page 65 shows that half in black, the difference between what the Palestinian Arabs were originally allocated and what they were left with after Israel's war on them. This missing half is never mentioned in later peace plans. The Israeli stance has always been that whatever the Arabs have now, the West Bank and Gaza, they should be prepared to give some of it to Israel for the sake of peace, and live in what is left. They should, in Israel's words, be prepared to 'compromise'. It is difficult to imagine a lexicon in which the word 'compromise' is used to describe a situation in which after 55% of its land was given away without consultation or consent, and another 23% stolen by force, the Palestinians should give yet more land to the people who stole the land in the first place.

Nevertheless, this absurdity is solemnly repeated with every set of peace negotiations.

Of course, the significant event I have not yet mentioned, and the one that most people assume is the reason there are peace talks at all, is the occupation of the remaining 22% by Israel after the Six Day War in 1967. This began as a result of what Israel described as a 'pre-emptive strike' to avoid – it said – being exterminated by the Egyptian army. In fact, this was a manufactured excuse. Ever since 1948, Israel leaders had said in private that they wanted more Arab land than they had been 'given' or already acquired by force. When Egypt mobilised its army in the Sinai desert, after cross-border tension, and closed the Straits of Tiran to Israeli shipping, Israel told its people that this was a grave threat to its existence and used it as an excuse to carry out a long-prepared plan to take over the West Bank and Gaza. As often happens in the Arab-Israeli dispute, Israel's justifications for its actions given at the time, often turn out to be fabricated excuses for public consumption with little or no connection with the truth.

In 1967, the entire story of the danger of extermination was invented in every detail and exaggerated *a posteriori* to justify the annexation of new Arab territory.

In case you think that sentence is too biased a statement, just put quotation marks around it and you have the words of Mordecai Bentov, a member of the Israel government at the time. (There are many other similar statements by Israeli soldiers and statesmen in later years.)

The Six Day War ended, as Israel intended, with the occupation of the rest of pre-1948 Palestine. In passing, it's worth drawing attention to the oddity of a state claiming to fear attack by another state taking its revenge by occupying the territory of a people who have nothing to do with the original *casus belli*. Punishing the Palestinians is Israel's spectator sport, and it will find any reason to do so.

But there's a deeper reason for this than just a deep-seated dislike of the Palestinians. It has been a constant theme of Zionist claims to Palestine that "the Arabs" have so much land that they should not begrudge the Jews a portion of it. By lumping together all nations which use Arabic and have ethnically Arab inhabitants, Israel can imply a homogeneity across the Arab world, with the implication that any member of any Arab nation is interchangeable with any other. In fact, of all the Arab nations, the Palestinians are the least able to threaten Israel militarily. So in order to continue the conflict, Israel has had to promote it as an Arab-Israeli conflict rather than admitting its true nature – the struggle of a dispossessed people for the return of its land.

It also suits Israel to deflect attention from the original dispossession of most of Palestine and only negotiate – or appear to negotiate – over the fate of the 22% that remains to the Palestinians. This is helped by the central place in all peace discussions of Security Council Resolution 242, passed by the United Nations in 1967.

This resolution called for "withdrawal of Israeli armed forces from territories occupied in the recent conflict", and "respect for and acknowledgement of the sovereignty, territorial integrity and political independence of every state in the area and their right to live in peace within secure and recognised boundaries free from threats or acts of force".

When the first serious efforts took place to address the conflict between Israel and the Palestinians in the 1970s, Resolution 242 was often used as a basis, as if, before 1967, everything had been sweetness and light between the two parties.

But of course before the Six Day War, Israel was already – according to one point of view – in possession of 50% of the land that had been allocated to the Palestinians in the Partition Plan, or – according to another point of view – it had turned the majority of the Arab land of Palestine into a Jewish state. All Palestinians held to one or other of these interpretations, and for them, this had to be the basis for any peace talks, not a discussion of whether Israel should be allowed to take over the remaining Palestinian land or not.

The Israeli stance in subsequent peace discussions has been to treat the 22% held by Palestinians as if it is the Palestinians' maximum demand and to call for 'compromise' over that land for the sake of peace. The Israelis have been helped in this approach by the unrepresentative nature of the Palestinian leadership over the years. Yasser Arafat was the first to accept that Resolution 242 should form the basis of any resolution of the territorial issues in the dispute, thus effectively granting to Israel not only the land that had been allocated to it under Partition but also the Palestinian land it had taken by force in 1948-9. From then on, the game was between successive teams of weak Palestinian negotiators, often leaned on by the US or Europe who were desperate to wash their hands of a problem they had helped to create, and a powerful, well-researched, heavily resourced Israeli team prepared to lie to obtain the maximum Israel could acquire of the remaining Palestinian land, preferably all of it.

To be fair to Arafat, having made a major concession over 242, which included the recognition of the "right of Israel to exist", he resisted all future attempts to hand over further areas of Palestinian land and to legitimize control of Jerusalem, to the frustration of leaders like Bill Clinton who thought they might go down in history as the solvers of the conflict. A major issue for Israel in such talks is that the growing population of illegal Israeli settlers in the West Bank, in 'settlements' which were actually large housing estates or new towns, meant that if they ever did have to give back West Bank land to the Palestinians they would have a devil of a job to move the settlers back to Israel. Even attempts by Israeli soldiers to move a dozen settlers from a ramshackle caravan site established as a 'settlement' led to huge protests in Israel and fighting between Israeli troops and Israeli citizens in the Occupied Territories.

In spite of most of the world's states parroting support for the Two-State Solution, no one has yet admitted the entire infeasibility of the idea, in the face of expanding settlements which day by day make such a solution more and more difficult to imagine. But then, that's why it's happening.

I think there is, and has been for a long time, the belief in Israel that time will solve the problem. After all, they say – inaccurately – 'we' waited 2000 years to 'return' to 'our' land. 'We' can surely wait a century or two longer until the Palestinians give up and slink away. The lie is given to this idea by the fact that, at its inception, Israeli governments believed that the Palestinians would soon give up and leave, particularly as the ones who weren't killed or expelled saw what happened to their compatriots and got out before they suffered in the same way. But they didn't. Particularly in the Galilee, where my ancestors came from, many villages and their inhabitants still remain as they were before 1948, albeit under a discriminatory Israeli administration. But at least it is better now than the military government they suffered in the few years after 1948, when they needed a permit to travel from one part of former Palestine to another.

So I suspect the main aim of any professed desire for peace that leads successive Israeli administrations to take part in 'peace talks' is to create a kind of placebo effect, where onlookers feel better because things look as if they are happening.

You only have to look at any aspect of the negotiations that have taken place over the years, and whose inner workings were revealed by participants in their memoirs, to realise how insincere the Israeli negotiators have been and how mendaciously they present the results when they – inevitably – fail.

Take Barak's 'most generous offer' to the Palestinians at the Camp David talks in 2000. Clinton who professed to be au fait with every detail of the situation convinced himself that this was a genuine and significant breakthrough in the negotiations. Here is what it consisted of:

Israel would 'retain' 9% of West Bank land, (land it was in possession of illegally.)

It would compensate Palestine for that loss by 'giving' it 1% of the land Israel illegally occupied in Gaza.

It would allow Palestine sovereignty over 85% of its border with Jordan. (In other words it would insist in controlling 15% of Palestine's border with Jordan.)

In East Jerusalem, illegally occupied, it would 'allow' Palestine sovereignty over seven out of nine neighbourhoods. (In other words, it would insist on Israeli sovereignty over two Arab neighbourhoods in East Jerusalem.)

In the Old City, the Muslim and Christian areas would come under Palestinian sovereignty, leaving Israel in control of the

Jewish and Armenian quarters. And the Haram al Sharif, the Muslim area with the Dome of the Rock and Al-Aqsa mosque, would be under joint custodianship of Palestine and Morocco.

Suppose I steal your four-storey house, and occupy the lower three floors, leaving you squashed into the top floor, with you having to pass my much better refurbished rooms every time you want to leave the house. Then one day, I move some members of my family into the top floor as well, where they proceed to order you around, take the rooms with the best view, and prevent you even going from one room to another. If I then offered to settle the dispute finally as long as you acknowledge my right to the three stories I occupied and let me keep one of the rooms on the top floor and let me control an area of the garden and give back only half of the best room in the house, you might not feel that was a 'generous offer.'

But for Clinton and Barak, this was exactly how they saw it.

Both Barak and Clinton had timetable and electoral problems at this stage in the Camp David talks and put extreme pressure on Arafat to say yes or no. With such an important issue as Jerusalem, Arafat needed time to consult other Muslim rulers, as well as to digest the elements of Barak's 'generous' plan. But Clinton insisted on a yes or no answer, and he got 'no'.

With a bit of further diddling around over the next few months and then the provocative trip to the Haram-al-Sharif by Ariel Sharon, leading to the Second Intifada, the Israelis got what they wanted: a Palestine that was clearly not 'a partner for peace' but an existential threat to Israel with its dozens of powerful teenage stone throwers who were more than a match for a few thousand soldiers with Uzis and a mere 1500 or so tanks and 6000 armoured personnel carriers.

The optimism with which supporters of a Two-State Solution promote the idea in the teeth of its evident impracticality can only be due to a lack of on-the-ground experience of the situation. When Mahmoud Abbas, the Palestinian president, showed George Bush a map of the West Bank and Gaza with Israeli checkpoints marked on it, Bush was astonished to see how they disrupted every journey Palestinians might want to make in the Occupied Territories. 'I thought that these checkpoints protected Israel from the Palestinian territory,' Bush said, 'and I find they are suffocating every Palestinian town and village.' As young people say these days 'duh…'.

Any Two-State Solution based on offers as 'generous' as Barak's will still lead to a Palestine riddled with checkpoints, to protect the settlers who would remain in the '9%'.

Such a Two-State Solution, with its continuing and permanent disruption to their daily life would be unacceptable to most Palestinians, but even if acceptance of that disruption could somehow be obtained, there is a much bigger gorilla in the room. A Two-State Solution with a Palestinian state in the West Bank and Gaza carries with it the abandonment of any claim to the rest of Palestine. That is what Israel would insist on. In fact, of course, there is no such feasible claim on the table by the Palestinians at the moment. Yasser Arafat gave that up when he recognised Israel within pre-1967 borders. But when he did that, neither he nor any other Palestinian suddenly revised their opinions about the events between 1917 and 1948. They still believe that Palestine was taken illegally from them with the help of the British and that Israel does not have a right to exercise sovereignty over it. Whatever agreement might be signed between a Palestinian leader who would be not much more than an Israeli puppet and an Israel puppet-master, delineating a so-called Two-State Solution, it would not change the mindset of Palestinians who would still await the day when they could travel and live in the land that was British Mandate Palestine. And if the Jews claim that they have waited 2000 years to 'return' why should the Palestinians give up any sooner?

Which brings me to the right of return.

Always in the background of any peace negotiations was the issue of the refugees. The 'generous offer' even included reference to the right of return for those Palestinian refugees and their descendants who were expelled in 1947-8 and 1967, one of the most contentious issues in the whole dispute. But all that Israel offered there was 'a satisfactory solution' to the refugee problem, with no further details. They can only have meant satisfactory to Israel, since nothing specific was on the table, and in all previous discussions the Israelis had refused to acknowledge that the refugee problem was anything to do with them, and certainly wasn't their fault. And of course, for the handful that might be allowed to return as a result of Israel's generosity most of them would not be returning to their original homes – which are now in Israel – but to a rump of pre-Mandate Palestine.

In the next chapter, I will address that issue.

5 Whose right of return?

The 'right of return' is a phrase which is frequently used to justify Jewish immigration to Palestine before 1948 and to Israel afterwards. It was codified in Israeli law in 1950 to allow Jews from anywhere in the world to become citizens of Israel. In fact, when it was passed it applied to persons of Jewish ancestry up to at least one Jewish grandparent and spouses of Jews, but was later widened. In 1970, the rights were "also vested in a child and a grandchild of a Jew, the spouse of a Jew, the spouse of a child of a Jew and the spouse of a grandchild of a Jew". As a result, there was an influx of new Israelis from Russia, some of them practising Orthodox Christians, and many of them not recognised as Jews at all by the Israeli religious authorities. In passing, it's ironic that people with no ethnic or religious connection with Palestine are encouraged to populate the country while its original inhabitants are kept out.

The phrase 'right of return' is an odd phrase to use in the case of world Jewry and Palestine. It is a good example of that English idiom about 'begging the question.' A statement that begs the question is one that slips in an unwarranted assumption while appearing to be about something else. The right of return seems to be about some right or other and the reader's attention is focused on that. But within the phrase the use of the word 'return' takes for granted that a Jew moving to Israel is in some sense 'returning', when in fact in most cases there is no evidence that he or she has been there before or, more important, that any of his or her ancestors ever set foot in the country.

What is galling for Palestinians, as they see the phrase being bandied around by Israel in its attempts to get more Jews to live in Israel (only a third or so of the world's Jews have chosen to take up the offer) is the fact that if anyone has a right to return, it is the Arab residents of Palestine whose unarguable lineage stretches back hundreds of years, and most of whom were expelled by Israel in 1948 and 1967, in a series of events called by Palestinians the *Nakba*, the catastrophe.

When they and their descendants go back to Palestine it will indubitably be a *return*, probably to a town or village with which they can demonstrate an ancestral connection, only a generation or two ago.

And not only will this be a genuine 'return' unlike the Jews who immigrate to Israel, it will also be taking up a 'right', one which is enshrined in natural law, as well as in UN Resolution 194 Para 11 which:

> Resolves that the refugees wishing to return to their homes and live at peace with their neighbours should be permitted to do so at the earliest practicable date, and that compensation should be paid for the property of those choosing not to return and for loss of or damage to property which, under principles of international law or in equity, should be made good by the Governments or authorities responsible...

One of the saddest 'what ifs' of the Israel-Palestine dispute is the issue of 'what if' the Swede, Count Folke Bernadotte, the

UN Security Council Mediator, had not been murdered as he was drawing up proposals for a definite conclusion to a peace deal in 1948. (And in fact, he was murdered because of those proposals.)

One of the elements of that deal was the following:

> "It is ... undeniable that no settlement can be just and complete if recognition is not accorded to the right of the Arab refugee to return to the home from which he has been dislodged by the hazards and strategy of the armed conflict between Arabs and Jews in Palestine. The majority of these refugees have come from territory which ... was to be included in the Jewish State. The exodus of Palestinian Arabs resulted from panic created by fighting in their communities, by rumours concerning real or alleged acts of terrorism, or expulsion. It would be an offence against the principles of elemental justice if these innocent victims of the conflict were denied the right to return to their homes while Jewish immigrants flow into Palestine, and, indeed, at least offer the threat of permanent replacement of the Arab refugees who have been rooted in the land for centuries.[7]

Bernadotte's 'rumours concerning ... terrorism' have become proven facts over the years as evidence of a deliberate attempt to kill and expel Palestinian villagers and townspeople has come to light. Ilan Pappé, one of the most diligent of the researchers into this issue, and an Israeli, has said:

> [There was a] "plan D" (Dalet), that reveals enough of the systematic expulsion. The idea was prepared by the Jewish military forces in March 1948. In that plan, they defined a very important principle: any Arab village or neighbourhood

---

[7] From the "Progress Report of the United Nations Mediator on Palestine by Folke Bernadotte. 16 September 1948. United Nations General Assembly Doc. A/648. Part one, section V, paragraph 6.

that would not surrender to the Jewish forces, that would not raise the white flag, would be uprooted, destroyed and the people expelled. I think they knew well that there was very little chance for more than five or six villages to surrender. Why should they surrender, especially after (the massacre of) Deir Yassin in April and the big fright in the Arab community? In fact, only four villages raised the white flag. All the rest were potentially an object of expulsion. I must add that a few other neighbourhoods raised the white flag but it didn't help them... All this is very clear. We have to remember that the UN partition plan of November 1947 would have left an equal number of Jews and Arabs in the Jewish state. This contradicted the idea of a Jewish state. So they had to make sure that as few Arabs as possible were still there. And that's what happened.[8]

David Ben-Gurion, first prime minister of Israel, put Jewish aims more succinctly in a letter to his son in 1937: "We must expel Arabs and take their place".[9]

Another Israeli historian, Benny Morris, accepted that there had been an incomplete attempt at 'ethnic cleansing', as it has been called, but said that if only it had been completed, there might have been peace today in the Middle East. (This seems an unlikely outcome unless every single Palestinian had been killed.) In reply, Professor Baruch Kimmerling of the Hebrew University in Jerusalem, said "If the Nazi programme for the final solution of the Jewish problem had been complete, for sure there would be peace today in Palestine."

Since Israel has never publicly accepted that it caused the Palestinian refugee problem, Bernadotte's recommendations to the UN had to be nipped in the bud, and a policy of 'kill

---

[8] http://msanews.mynet.net/MSANEWS/199912/19991205.0.html

An Interview of Ilan Pappe By Baudouin Loos Brussels, 29 November 1999

[9] Quoted in Journal of Palestine Studies, Vol. 41, No. 2 (Winter 2012), pp. 245-250

the messenger' was adopted. On 17th September 1948, Bernadotte was murdered by a gang of three Israeli Jews, ordered to carry out their task by a terrorist called Yitzhak Shamir who led the Jewish terror group, Lehi, and had previously arranged the assassination of a British politician, Lord Moyne. Fifteen years later, Shamir became prime minister of Israel.

Israel's denial of responsibility for the expulsion of Palestinians and theft of their property continues into the 21st century. Here is a typical example of the continuing mendacity of Israel's campaign of 'hasbara', a propaganda campaign aimed at the West to falsify the origins and actions of the Israeli state:

> As a result of the 1948 war, Israel absorbed some 600,000 Jewish refugees from all over the Arab world, and about the same number of Arabs left Israel.[10]

Taken from an online 'journal of politics and the arts', this statement is typical of the daily lies propagated about the Palestinians and, to be fair, believed as truth by many Jewish supporters of Israel because they seek no other sources of information.

'Leaving' a country implies a degree of volition that was entirely absent from the Nakba. And, by the way, many of the Jewish 'refugees', particularly from Morocco and Iraq, were coerced by Zionist enforcers into leaving countries and homes they had lived in for generations in order to boost the Jewish population of the new state of Israel, in the face of a lack of enthusiasm from many European Jews who preferred to seek sanctuary in the US, Canada or the UK rather than start a new life in a dusty, hot Middle Eastern state. In Iraq, for example,

---

[10] Talia Einhorn, *The status of Palestine/land of Israel and its settlement under public international law*, Nativ online, vol.1/2003, a journal of politics and the arts

many Jews left for Israel after five bombs were planted, in the US Information Service offices and in synagogues in Baghdad. Years later it came to light that the bombs were all organised by the Israeli intelligence agency, Mossad, in order to destroy the 110,000-strong Jewish community in Iraq, which had lived there peacefully for generations.

For Palestinians, the denial of responsibility by Israel for their losses is contradicted by every piece of evidence that exists, and anything that appears to support the Zionist narrative usually turns out to have been fabricated.

To take one small example, for a long time after 1948, Israel maintained that many Arabs left of their own free will, encouraged by broadcasts from Arab radio stations. Assiduous research over the years has failed to find any evidence to support this, although many pro-Israel websites and books repeat the statement as if it was fact.

The case that Israel deliberately expelled and sometimes killed Palestinians only grows stronger as more archives are opened. It is difficult not to stumble on evidence like this cable addressed by Major General Carmel to all division and district commanders on October, 31, 1948:

> Do all you can to immediately and quickly purge the conquered territories of all hostile elements in accordance with the orders issued. The residents should be helped to leave the areas that have been conquered.[11]

'Hostile elements' is an interesting phrase. Who would not be hostile to a foreign army which invades your village, a village in territory allocated to the Arabs in the Partition plan. You are unlikely to welcome them with open arms and throw flowers. And if you don't welcome them, you are a 'hostile element' and your village can be 'purged.' Evidence of the

---

[11] M.B. Qumsiyeh, 20 Zionist Myths Exposed,
http://www.iap.org/zioinism19.htm [sic]

expulsions which actually took place shows that this phrase was far from referring to people with guns. Men, women and children were forced to leave their homes with only what they could carry, and forbidden from ever returning.

The Nakba is not just a case of losses in wartime, where both sides suffer. Instead, it was a deliberate attempt to change the terms of the UN Partition proposal, something Israel only accepted in order to get a foothold in Palestine, so that as few Arabs as possible remained in the Jewish state.

Against this background, the right of Palestinians finally to return to Palestine if they want to is difficult to deny. It has been raised as part of every attempt to settle the dispute, and rejected every time by Israel. Apart from denying any responsibility for Palestinian losses, Israel also says it hasn't room for any returning Palestinians in spite of the fact that it would be happy to admit another fifteen million Jews if they chose to settle.

The most Israel has ever been willing to consider as part of a peace agreement, and this probably under extreme pressure from the Americans, is the return of a token number, maybe 5,000, maybe as many as 25,000, to what is now Israel, and the rest to the West Bank and Gaza. And of course, this would be offered as a good will gesture rather than any acceptance of responsibility for their losses in the first place.

Analogies taken from nearer to home are helpful in these circumstances. Suppose three quarters of the population of the UK had been expelled by the Germans in 1945, after an unexpected victory over the Allies, which led to the Germans turning Britain into a German state, apart from Wales, where some UK citizens had managed to escape to or remain in. Suppose, after 70 years a peace deal was negotiated, which allowed a return to the UK for those survivors and their descendants, now in refugee camps in France and Spain and Denmark, or settled further afield in the US or Canada. And suppose the return was confined to Wales, for anyone who had lived anywhere in the UK. Scots, northerners, Cornishmen, Londoners, all would be offered permission to live in Wales but nowhere else in the new German state. Someone whose family lived in Shrewsbury, for example, would only be allowed to live in Welshpool, less than 20 miles away. (This is analogous with friends of mine born and brought up in Jerusalem, who now live in Ramallah, eleven miles away, and are banned from ever visiting the city of their birth and upbringing.) The Shrewsbury native would at least be in similar countryside and could almost 'see' their home in the distance. But for a Yorkshireman or a Scot, what sort of return would this be?

This is similar to the contemptuous 'offer' included in some peace agreements: a quarter of one percent to return to ancestral villages and towns, the rest to cram into the West Bank and Gaza, an area which is already crowded, underresourced and often very different in terrain and economy from the places from which Palestinians were expelled.

The Palestinian 'right of return' is one that is enshrined in international law as codified by UN Resolutions, and, unlike the Jewish right of return, has a clarity and sense of justice about it. Certainly the world 'return' has a much more concrete and verifiable meaning for individual Palestinians than any Jew elsewhere in the world who considers taking up the offer.

For the oldest living generation of Palestinians, returning to Palestine would be travelling back to a country in which he or she once lived. For later generations, it would be returning to a country in which he or she had lived as a child, or travelling to a place in which he or she would have lived if the family had not been unjustly expelled. In each case, unlike the Jewish right of return, being offered the opportunity to live again in the territory that was Palestine would be a personal right connecting an individual somewhere in the world outside Palestine with a place in Palestine.

Part 2
The Plan

—

Part 2: The Plan

Let me start by saying two things:

1. Parts of this plan have been common currency among many Palestinian supporters of the One-State Solution. But the combination of elements I present in this book has not been spelled out in this way before.

2. However, I have mentioned the outline of it to a range of knowledgeable Palestinians and incorporated their comments and reactions where I agreed with them.

But it is true to say that obtaining agreement to every element, even from the Palestinians, will not be easy. And of course, "the Israelis" by which I mean the people who currently represent them, will see this plan as representing everything they have been trying to avoid for the last 70 years. But I am not particularly concerned about that. There are two ways in which this plan can become acceptable to Israelis. Either enough ordinary citizens of Israel realise that they have reached the end of the road under a succession of vicious, racist right-wing governments, and elect a government which will see this plan as win-win for everyone. Or there will be concerted action by major powers to enforce this plan on Israel as it is now, through sanctions, withdrawal of aid, dismantling of security arrangements and so on, which will probably have the same effect as leading to a government that genuinely wants what's best for all the citizens between the Jordan and the Mediterranean.

6 The single state

The plan I am exploring is dependent not only on the right to return to Palestine but also on there being a Palestine to return to which bears some relation to the homes and communities from which Palestinians were expelled in 1947-9. The only solutions that have been explored formally between the various parties with an interest in the area envisage a Palestine that is a rump of the original country, 22%. Redefining a much larger area to which Palestinians could return suddenly removes a number of obstacles that prevented Palestinians considering any previous plans raised at the numerous discussions from Madrid to Camp David, since they were so far from what natural justice required.

The idea of a single state for Israelis and Palestinians is a simple one to describe, and – many people would say – impossible to execute.

In this chapter, I will state the idea at its simplest, rather than address directly the complex issues which may stand in the way of achieving it. But I will come at those ideas indirectly by using a technique used in a book called Objections to *Christian Belief* published in 1963 in which four leading Christians justified Christianity by addressing, and hoping to dismiss, major objections to it.

First, my definition:

The One-State solution to the Palestine-Israel dispute is to set up one democratic state for all its citizens, between the Jordan and the Mediterranean, in which no race, creed or social group has privileged status, and all citizens have equal national and political rights.

It is an idea which, when promoted early in the 21st century, most notably by Edward Said, was very unfashionable, because in those years it was possible to cling to the possibility that there might be two states, Israel and Palestine, coexisting side by side in the area of Mandate Palestine. Now, of course, as the Two-State Solution disappears into the dustbin of history, by default the One-State Solution is the only one that is left, as a result of decisions made by Israel to infiltrate Israeli citizens, communities and infrastructure throughout the West Bank so that there is no possibility of a contiguous state of Palestine side by side with Israel.

Even within Israel and among some of the supporters of the Two-State Solution, the One-State idea is increasingly discussed, usually dangled as a threat, an outcome to be avoided at all costs but which might happen unless the current Israeli government makes more effort to come to an agreement with the Palestinians.

Here is a quote from 2016 which is typical of the growing realisation that this may be the only solution.

> The Peace Process is dead. The next US President will have to deal with an Israel determined to permanently occupy all the territory between the Jordan River and the Mediterranean Sea, including where 2.5 million West Bank Palestinians live. How did we get there? So many people stuck knives into the peace process it's hard to know who delivered the mortal blow. Was it the fanatical Jewish settlers determined to keep expanding their footprint in the West Bank and able to sabotage any Israeli politician or

army officer who opposed them? Was it right wing Jewish billionaires, like Sheldon Adelson, who used their influence to blunt any US Congressional criticism of Bibi Netanyahu? Or was it Netanyahu, whose lust to hold on to his seat of power is only surpassed by his lack of imagination to find a secure way to separate from the Palestinians?"

This is all good so far, then the writer goes on to blame the PA and Hamas as well, for having the temerity to resist Israel's illegal occupation of the West Bank and its stranglehold on Gaza. The writer finishes:

They all killed the two-state solution. Let the one-state era begin. It will involve a steady low-grade civil war between Palestinians and Israelis and a growing Israeli isolation in Europe and on college campuses that the next US President will have to navigate.

That was written in the *New York Times* by an American journalist called Tom Friedman, who has not been known as a friend to Palestine or the Palestinians, and the fact that even he has seen the writing on the wall and written in his paper about it is quite a significant statement. For a Jewish-American journalist, who has often accepted the Zionist claim to Palestine, to recognise that the Israelis are (even partly) responsible for the death of the peace process is a major step forward.

In talking and writing about One Democratic State I have encountered seven main objections to the idea.

The first one is that **'Israel won't allow it.'**

It is almost always the first objection which is offered, and often seen as so devastating that it's not worth talking about the topic any more.

But when does anybody go into a negotiation accepting the fact that the other party is not going to allow certain things – in this case the key point – and therefore abandoning it?

The issue is not so much whether Israel today would allow it. If current and future Israeli governments behave in the future as they have in the past – that is, impose such one-sided conditions on Palestinians as a requirement for negotiations that they know no Palestinian government would have a popular mandate to enter them – the matter will be taken out of their hands once it becomes apparent that the One-State Solution is the only option with a chance of bringing the conflict to an end.

I believe that whoever takes part in these negotiations – whichever future government of Israel is in power – will be constrained to take the ODS idea seriously, and will come to the realisation that there is no other way out but to explore this idea.

We have seen enough problems on the international scene which seemed insoluble until they were solved, to realise that you should never say 'never' in international politics. Who would have thought that the Soviet Union could collapse? Who would have thought that East Germany would crumble? Who would have thought that South Africa would stop being an apartheid state? In each of those situations, somebody thinking about the situation before these dramatic changes occurred could dismiss any likelihood of the eventual outcomes by saying 'the Soviet government, the East German government, the white South African government wouldn't accept it'. Well, of course, *those* governments never did accept the changes, but other governments emerged which did.

The trouble with the One State idea is that people often can't really understand how to get there and because they can't understand that, they think it's unachievable.

But my stance is that you start by conceiving the best end point, best in the sense of bringing justice to Palestinians and Israelis, and then all parties have to accept that that is the aim, and you work through how best to achieve that aim.

Israel today is different from Israel forty years ago, and could be different from Israel in ten or twenty years' time. I can envisage a situation in which the benefits of a single state, even for Israelis, outweigh the perceived disadvantages – not least the never-ending and possibly increasing hostility of most of the rest of the world – and may lead to a change in the views and ideas of Israeli voters. And there is another possibility, which – perhaps – if future Israeli governments are as obdurate as current ones, will be the only answer. The major powers have united against Iran and imposed sanctions which seem to be leading to an abandonment of its nuclear weapons programme. If Israel continued to elect the type of racist right-wing government we have seen in recent decades, which refused to negotiate with the Palestinians, I can imagine a situation in which, led by a different US president, there would be a change of government in Israel which is interested in peace and justice and which might even welcome a shared government over a larger territory, with fewer security problems, a smaller military budget, the end of the settlement headache and increased prosperity from the influx of money and skilled people that the right of return scheme would produce.

The second objection often raised to ODS is that **'it would change the Jewish nature of the state'.**

To explore this we need to look deeper at what that actually means. Since Israel defines itself as 'the Jewish state', presumably this objection relates to some dilution of the Jewishness of Israel, a dilution which must exist already since 20% of the population is either Muslim or Christian. But Israel is in a bind – or would be if its politicians ever thought rationally – because the same Israelis who insist on everyone accepting it as the Jewish state also accuse people of anti-semitism who describe its actions, for example, its many crimes against the Palestinians, as 'Jewish'.

There is a sense, of course, in which ODS *would* change the Jewish nature of the state and that would be no bad thing. Israel is an anachronism, a state which professes to be a member of the modern community of nations and yet whose underlying governance is racist and strongly connected with a set of religious rules derived from the practices of a small group of Judeans 2,500 years ago, and their fundamentalist beliefs. A recent book, *Politically Incorrect*, by Ofra Yeshua-Lyth gives a detailed account of the state-sanctioned imposition of religious rules and conventions, to do with marriage and birth and death and child-rearing, on large swathes of the Israeli population who do not observe the Jewish religion, and would prefer a secular life. Statistics of the number of Israelis who order kosher food on El Al flights suggests that at least 50% of Israelis – at least those who fly – are non-observant, and yet suffer from the constraints of a Judaism-dominated system of government.

Clearly these are not serious religious Jews; they're citizens of Israel, and they're presumably people for whom their Jewishness is a cultural artefact, rather than a deep religious belief.

So, the idea that the nature of the state might be changed in the One Democratic State could be welcomed by many Jews who would live in the new state but who would no longer lead lives determined by the extreme religious bodies that keep right wing governments in power. These would include some of the million or so Russians who immigrated to Israel after the collapse of the Soviet Union, many of whom were in any case Orthodox Christians but benefitted from a relaxation of the rules defining who is a Jew.

Since in the new state there would be protection of religious beliefs and removal of the kind of discrimination that exists in Israel at the moment, no Jew who wanted to practice his religion would be prevented from doing so. Nor would any Israeli who wanted a non-religious marriage or burial, or balked at subjecting her baby son to the painful mutilation of circumcision, be prevented from leading the life of her choice. I could even envisage – if enough Jews wanted it – the establishing of a Jewish cultural centre which the Jews of the world could visit to recharge their spiritual or cultural batteries. It could be like the 'national home' promised by the Balfour Declaration, which, in public, British politicians and political Zionists denied was intended to be a Jewish state and said that it would be merely a spiritual centre of some sort. Such a centre would not be a separate enclave with privileges that aren't available to the other citizens, but some means by which those Jews in the rest of the world who are sincerely religious could have a connection with the state, and not feel that their own religious ideas were neglected or ignored. Since two thirds of the world's Jewish population seem to be happy living outside Israel, they would have a connection with the country that did not involve giving up a settled life in America, Britain or Europe.

A third objection I hear a lot is **'Arabs and Jews are historical enemies and will continue to fight each other.'**

Two nights before writing this I spoke at a meeting in an Oxford college, and raised the issue of the One State Solution. The moderator, who knows far more about the Middle East than I do, said "But won't there be immediate violence? The extreme Zionists are not going to accept a state which no longer has an exclusive Jewish character and will attack the Arabs." Usually when this objection is raised, it is based on the belief that, given half a chance and access to the whole of Palestine without an army of occupation in some of it, the Palestinian Arabs will go on the rampage in the way my Oxford friend envisaged with many Jews in the new state.

It surprises me how many people believe that the hostility we now see between Arabs and the Jewish citizens of Israel somehow goes back hundreds of years, that it's in their genes. In fact, in the early part of the twentieth century, before political Zionism came into Palestine, Arabs and Jews were not at each other's throats. My family has stories of Jewish friends down the road who babysat for them, who played tric-trac together and smoked the nargileh, and so on. What people don't realise is that it was precisely the influx of political Zionists and the fear that the Palestinians were going to lose their state and their freedom and their privileges, which generated the suspicion, aggression and hostility. And history shows that they were right to be suspicious. Politician after politician denied that the intention of the Balfour Declaration was to change Palestine into a Jewish state while, by their actions, that's what they did.

The Palestinians have suffered at the hands of Israel and its founders, and in this new state one wouldn't blame people for feeling animosity towards those Jews who have been instrumental in their oppression. Many thousands of

Palestinians have lost relatives and friends as a result of the actions of the Israel Defense Forces. It is also, of course, true that those Israelis who have lost relatives and friends by the actions of the various militant Palestinian groups will, as they have always done, associate these events with all Palestinians. It is also possible that, as my Oxford friend feared, former Israeli Jews in the new state will allow their racism and bigotry to get the better of any ideas of abiding by the new constitution of the state.

But I believe that, provided a constitution is created for the new state in which none of the religious or cultural groups – Christians, Muslims or Jews – feel that the other is more privileged, the hostility that we've seen as a result of the Zionist, British and Israeli actions would not continue in the new state, or would disappear after a few years. Of course, there will always be crime in any state, and all we can work for is to construct for the new state a fair judicial system and an unbiased police force.

But I have also heard the objection, related to the previous one, that **'no constitution could be devised which would be acceptable to all citizens of the new state.'**

Well, there are governments around the world, in which different groups – religious groups, national groups, linguistic groups – live in the same country and share the government. It's not been an unalloyed success in Belgium, let's say, or Yugoslavia, although Switzerland is a better example. Lebanon is a country where a constitution designed to share power between communities has sometimes worked.

But there is an extra factor in the case of the governance of this new country which I think could make a huge difference. If ODS were to happen, if an agreement in principle was to be made, there would be a huge amount of good will in the rest of the world to try and make it happen. At the moment, people who support Israel or Palestine are clearly on opposite sides of the fence. If there was some possibility that the Jews and the Palestinians would come together, and share a government of the state, there would be a huge effort by the United Nations and by different countries around the world, to lend advice – legal advice, constitutional advice, and security advice – to help make it happen, monitor the new constitution in operation and bring healing to the longest running sore in world politics.

It would not be the case that on Day One of the new state all these new citizens would be left to sort themselves out. I think it would clearly require a lot of work, a lot of collaboration, and a lot of support from the rest of the world, but considering the amount of time and energy the Arab-Israel conflict takes up, the time taken up in the United Nations by consideration of the conflict, the lives that are lost, when you think of the possibility all this might stop, it would be a great encouragement to the nations of the world to try and make it happen.

Another question people ask is '**what would happen to the Israeli settlements?'**

It has been shown over the years of Israel's illegal settlement-building in the West Bank and Gaza that the slightest effort by the Israeli government to remove tiny settlements that, even by their own biased laws, are illegal, is met with violent and abusive resistance by the settlers who claim all of Palestine as their own territory.

But unlike with the Two-State solution, in the One Democratic State, the illegal settlements cease to be a problem. If everybody living between the Jordan and the Mediterranean is a citizen of the new state, this will include the settlers. They wouldn't be asked to move from their settlements and could stay in the West Bank if they wanted. Of course, all sorts of other things would change about the settlements. They would no longer be fenced, with armed guards; there would no longer be special roads which only they could use; there would be no more government subsidies to encourage or maintain the construction and running of settlements. And indeed, one might find that some of the settlers just didn't want to stay any more. If they had come to Israel in search of an apartheid state to live in, where they wouldn't have to have any contact with Arabs, they would either have to abandon that illusion or abandon their home and return to where they were born and brought up. And I don't think many of the citizens of the new state would be heartbroken if that was what happened.

But the fact is, in the ODS nobody would have to move anywhere, though they might choose to. Nor could the former Israelis have the privileged status they have at the moment. They couldn't have access to a disproportionate amount of water from West Bank aquifers, for example. A third of Israel's water comes from the West Bank. It takes ("steals") 93% of it, leaving 7% for the Palestinians. The per capita consumption by Israelis is three times what Palestinians consume, and Israeli agriculture uses 10 times per capita. With One Democratic State, such figures would become meaningless. Water from all sources would be shared equally, since there could be no Jewish taps and Arab taps in the Single State.

If a settlement house became vacant in the future, it could be sold or lived in by Arabs or Jews and there would be the sort of housing market found in the rest of the world with no discrimination of the sort that goes on in Israel and Palestine at the moment. There would be changes which former settlers would see as inconveniences if they stayed, but in principle, the settlements would not have to be dismantled. They would just have to be de-securitised, if there is such a word, and made open in the way Arab villages in the West Bank are.

Another objection that is raised is that **'the Single State would not be economically viable.'** Perhaps this is based on thoughts of the costs of merging two systems, pouring money and resources into the West Bank and Gaza, dismantling the security fence, reuniting Jerusalem, reconstructing the administration, civil service and so on.

But we are not talking about a state which will have to be self-financing from the beginning. As part of the response of the rest of the world to the prospect of a more peaceful Middle East, there would be a lot of aid forthcoming to ensure that the new state gets off to a good start. America gives a lot of 'aid' at the moment to Israel, $38 billion over ten years, although it is hardly a third world country that couldn't earn its way in the world. If you combine amounts like that with funding from the World Bank, the IMF, the EU and the Arab world as part of a ten-year plan to get the new state on its feet, the issue of economic viability looks a bit less of a problem.

Some people say, '**a single state for Arabs and Jews would be replacing an injustice to the Palestinians with an injustice to the Israelis.**' It depends on how you define injustice. I think the Israelis have had a disproportionate amount of benefit from taking over the Palestinians' land and the Palestinians have had a disproportionate amount of suffering from losing their land. So a single state would be seen as redressing that imbalance.

And, indeed, I'm not sure what sense of injustice a Jewish Israeli would feel in the new state if he or she still lived in the same house, went to the same shops, and had the same friends. It is true that some Jewish Israelis might resent or see it as unjust that they have to live with or be near to Arabs in a way that they hadn't before, but I'm sure they can learn to live with it.

It would only seem unjust for those Israelis who want to live in an exclusively Jewish state, which will no longer be possible.

One issue that is often raised about Israel is that it is a "haven for the Jews". On the evidence of immigration over the last hundred years, it seems to me that most of the Jews who need such a haven have already emigrated there. The last year for which I have figures, 2015, shows one immigrant per thousand population, compared with an average of fifteen or so at previous five-year intervals. The fact is that two-thirds of the world's Jews have chosen to live outside Israel, and I suspect that will not change much.

There is obviously and genuinely some kind of psychological benefit for those Jews who have no intention of moving to Israel in thinking that they could, one day, if necessary, if the world turned against them. But I think that is one factor too many to have to consider in the future of this area. We can't deprive the Palestinians of rights which they have been without for a hundred years because of a psychological feeling that Jews in the diaspora would like to have.

So the One Democratic State idea is the first part of my plan. The second part, which needs the first to make the whole plan successful, is the Right of Return for all Palestinian Arabs.

7   The right of return

As with the concept of the Single State, I am going to define what I mean by the Right of Return for Palestinians quite simply. But as will become clear it is not at all a simple concept, or rather it can be expressed simply but there is plenty of scope for people who want to make it complicated.

The claim made by Palestinians that they have a right to return to the homes they and their ancestors lived in before 1948 is supported – but was not created – by UN resolution 194, passed in December 1948, near the end of the Arab-Israeli War.

As mentioned on page 74 this says that:

> [R]efugees wishing to return to their homes and live at peace with their neighbours should be permitted to do so at the earliest practicable date, and ... compensation should be paid for the property of those choosing not to return and for loss of or damage to property which, under principles of international law or equity, should be made good by the Governments or authorities responsible.

Six months later, Israel passed a law which has become known as the right of return, which gives the right to "Jews" to come and live in Israel and acquire Israeli citizenship. The reason I have put "Jews" in quotes is that "Who is a Jew?" is a question which is given different answers by different people and entities and at different times.[12] In fact, even Israeli lawmakers have changed their minds over time, today allowing someone who is the grandchild of a Jew or married to a Jew to shelter under the Jewish umbrella when they were not included before.

The Palestinian right of return is a very different concept. There, the two words 'right' and 'return' have very different meanings from the Jewish 'right of return'. First, the Jewish 'right' is created by a state as part of its system of laws. States can decide who to offer citizenship to, without there being any natural or basic right involved. Israel could offer citizenship to redheads or footballers, without blondes or cricketers having an occasion to complain about being omitted.

In the case of Palestinians, they are not basing their claim on a law passed by someone authenticating their right to return to Palestine. They are not even basing it on UN Resolution 194, although they use that to point out – as one example of many – that Israel ignores scores of UN resolutions which it doesn't like. Their claim goes deeper. It is the same right that allows me to resist having my house taken over by vagabonds, and that – if I am kidnapped and taken to another place – allows me to return and expel the vagabonds with the full support of the forces of the law.

Israel could pass a law tomorrow denying citizenship to all non-Israeli Jews, and no one would bat an eyelid, or at least no one could say that this was a breach of the human rights of non-Israeli Jews. But no one could pass a law saying that

---

[12] An excellent book by Gilad Atzmon, called *The Wandering Who?* shows what an ill-formed and sometimes self-contradictory concept Jewishnness is. Also, see *The Invention of the Jewish People*, by Shlomo Sand.

from now on, a Palestinian expelled from his house in 1948, or even a Palestinian who left it for a time to avoid the dangers of war, no longer had any *rights* in that house. Of course, Israel has passed laws which ban Palestinians from returning, even as visitors, but that does not affect one whit their right to return.

Arrangements for a right of return will start with the issuing of a passport for all Palestinians and their descendants, granting to them citizenship of the new state. This citizenship carries with it the same rights of property ownership and place of residence as all other citizens of the state, some of whom will be former Israelis and others former inhabitants of the West Bank and Gaza.

In addition to citizenship, everyone agrees (apart from most Jewish Israelis) that there should be some sort of package that in some form provides the necessary arrangements and funding for those Palestinians who wish to return to Palestine. There have been suggestions in the past as to ways in which this might happen, but the Palestine to which the right of return has applied has been the territory of a putative Palestinian state side by side with Israel.

Nevertheless, such plans have included two main elements, compensation for loss, and restitution of residency and citizenship, and my plan has the same two elements, with the residency component subdivided in a way which may help with the resolution of the conflict.

Here is what I suggest:

A. A sum of money in full compensation for loss of property and for suffering endured over decades, to be paid to all Palestinians, but with a larger amount going to older Palestinians, for reasons explained below.

B1. A guaranteed house or apartment as near as possible to the town, village or area from which their family came, for those who wish to return to the new state to live permanently.

OR

B2. The opportunity to remain in their country of residence but return for a set period each year, reserved on a 'timeshare' basis, to specially constructed resorts in the part of Palestine from which their family came, where all travel and accommodation expenses would be covered by the Right of Return scheme. This would provide a connection to Palestine, and the opportunity to meet other Palestinians from the same area, without necessarily uprooting from the place the refugees have lived in for many years.

There are probably a hundred questions that arise in the mind of somebody reading this for the first time, particularly if they already have some knowledge of the Palestine-Israel situation.

Here are a few to get started:

- How could you fit them all in?
- How much would it all cost?
- Would every Palestinian get the same amount of compensation?
- Where would all the money come from?
- Wouldn't you have to expel a lot of Jewish Israelis from their homes?
- Would all Palestinians agree to such a scheme?
- What sort of infrastructure would be necessary to put the Right of Return into operation?
- What evidence would be needed to qualify?
- How could you be sure that only Palestinians were applying?

Answering some of these questions is what the rest of this book is about.

But first, what sort of uptake would there be of these options? Would all Palestinians want to return? Or all take compensation? Or, most likely, a whole range of choices between these two?

To start with, I need to emphasise that the options offered to Palestinian refugees should be based on right not on need. I do not have any time for someone who says "why should a rich Palestinian living in London be given the same compensation, in cash or kind, as a poor Palestinian who has lived all her life in the deprived community of a refugee camp in Lebanon?" The rich Palestinian and his family in London has suffered the same loss as the poor Palestinian in the camp. They were both deprived of home, heritage and dignity by Israel and have had their claims ignored and denigrated over the decades.

The different groups of Palestinians may differ in their responses to the new plan. Those who are nearest to their original homes – refugees in camps around the current Israeli border, and those who have established lives and citizenships in Lebanon, Syria, Jordan and Egypt – may be most interested in opting for a full, funded return as near as possible to their original homes. The people in the camps have kept alive family and village relationships and if they returned in large numbers those relationships could be preserved in places which some of them still remember and others have heard much about. Of those who have made careers and new lives in Beirut or Amman or Damascus, perhaps the older members would return to live in the places they remember while the younger ones would take the "timeshare" option, knowing that, with passports for the new state, they could return whenever they like either to visit or to settle.

Of those who live in the West Bank or Gaza, there are likely to be various priorities determining what they opt for. A well-off family living in Ramallah or Nablus, whether or not they came originally from that part of Palestine, would be likely to decide to stay where they are. In the new state, if they decided to stay put, wherever they came from in pre-1948 Palestine they would be within a couple of hours' drive of their ancestral home, just as someone born in Birmingham has no qualms about working and living in London, because he knows he can always get on a train or drive back to his family home.

However, someone living in a village house in the West Bank who had arrived there having been expelled from his home village in what is currently Israel, perhaps deprived today by Israeli laws of planning permission, adequate water and poor power supplies might decide for the sake of a clean break to return to the ancestral home area, and take up the offer of a new house, and the accompanying benefits.

Moving further afield, fewer Palestinians living in the west, having established new homes and lives, might be interested in a full return, which would disrupt their lives and those of their families, and they might merely take the 'timeshare' option. However, it is worth saying that the talents of those who have become doctors, businessmen, educators, academics, architects, tradesmen and so on will all be needed in the new state, for two reasons.

First, of course, the increase in population will create a demand for increased facilities, particular in the construction sector. Both the 'timeshare' option and the new houses needed for those who take up residence will generate a massive demand for the skills and talents of Palestinians from abroad.

Second, although no one would wish it, it may be the case that there would be some emigration of Jewish Israelis, many of whom have dual nationality anyway, who can't stomach the idea of sharing Palestine with its original inhabitants. The skills and talents of those Jews who emigrate will also need to be replaced. Although I wouldn't rule out the possibility that, for some non- or anti-Zionist Jews, the new state will be more attractive – and more secure – than Israel is at present and that there will be inward migration but controlled by a more restricted law of return for Jews.

For most Palestinians who have established lives and careers outside Palestine, I believe the most attractive option will be the 'timeshare' option. The freedom to visit Palestine with their families, to meet – by arrangement or by chance encounter – other Palestinians from the same area, will be an attractive one, and this will be available to all Palestinians, whichever option they choose. But if they also choose to take advantage of free accommodation, food and travel to Palestine every year if they want, this will be a powerful incentive for families to strengthen ties with Palestine and perhaps lead to future generations of young Palestinians returning permanently or creating a connection with their ancestral land that is not possible at the moment, because of Israel's ban on expatriate Palestinians even visiting Palestine.

8 The Details

shall now go into a little more detail, not in order to be definitive but to show how many different issues will be raised once a scheme is set up.

Compensation

I define a Palestinian as follows: Anyone of Arab descent who lived in Palestine before 1948 or can demonstrate a family connection with pre-1948 Palestine. A family connection means the child or grandchild of someone who possessed, or was entitled to, Palestinian citizenship under the British Mandate.

There could be two categories for the purpose of compensation calculation:

A: Palestinians who lived in pre-1948 Palestine for a year or more.
B: Descendants of A.

Each Palestinian will be entitled to a lump sum in compensation. He or she would also be entitled to citizenship of the new state. These would be in full and final settlement of the losses and distress caused by the Nakba (but would not include the costs of return.) I suggest that Palestinians in group B should receive less in compensation than those in group A. In all conscience, my losses, for example, are losses of opportunity, whereas my father's and his brothers' and sisters' were denial of nationality, identity, respect and, in some cases, relatives.

The lump sum compensation amounts will be the same for everyone in each of these two groups. In addition, all Palestinians will be offered one or other of the following forms of residence in the new state:

Rehousing

A. In the original family house.
B. In similar accommodation in the original family village, town or suburb. (The overwhelming majority of refugees would be able to return to currently empty sites.[13])
C. In one of the 'New Villages' to be built on the site of, or in a similar landscape to, the major centres of Arab habitation on pre-1948 Palestine, many of which were destroyed by Israel.

These houses/flats would be free and the Palestinian(s) would own them, and could receive an annual income for a fixed period, maybe five or ten years, along with house maintenance costs for the life of the returner(s). These residences would be converted old houses or specially built new developments, architect-designed and well-equipped. In a very few situations it might be possible to return to the actual family houses from which Palestinians were expelled, and every effort would be made to achieve this. Certainly,

---

[13] http://www.plands.org/en/books-reports/books/right-of-return-sacred-legal-and-possilble/location-of-palestinian-villages

they should be allowed to return to the villages or towns from which they came. This is particularly important when these places are among the several hundred destroyed by the Israelis after 1948. In some ways, it would be easier to return to the site of a destroyed community, to be rebuilt in a similar style and with similar neighbourhoods, than to deal with the problems of a formerly Arab town that was taken over by Jewish immigrants. Such a town is Safad, where my father's family came from.

Families will be expected to make their best efforts to consolidate their claims. In other words, where possible, members of the same family will be encouraged to share accommodation rather than each member claim entirely separate residences. But it will not be a requirement of their return that they do so.

Clearly, in only a few cases will Option A be possible, either because the houses are now lived in by other residents, or the houses or villages have been destroyed. But as part of the scheme, existing residents will be offered compensation if they choose to move out to make way for the original owners.

Option B will not always be possible either, because many villages were destroyed by Israel after 1948. But as part of the Return Programme, many of the destroyed villages will be reconstructed, as far as possible in a style and layout which matches the original community, with enhanced modern facilities. A major six-year project instituted by the Palestine Land Society is already under way to design individual villages on the sites of many destroyed Palestinian villages.

In each of these cases, all the costs of construction, purchase, adaptation or renovation would be covered by the Right of Return programme, along with an annual income and lifetime running costs of the residence.

"Timesharing"

This is an element of a projected scheme which I have not

seen described elsewhere. This doesn't mean no one has suggested it, or that it hasn't been considered and rejected as either impractical or culturally irrelevant. I would only say that, as someone who, under my definition, would qualify for the right of return, it is a very attractive option for me and my family. This is how it would work:

Palestinians choosing this option would be entitled every year to a number of weeks' free accommodation, food and other benefits, (I suggest between two and four weeks) along with car hire for the period, in one of a number of newly built or renovated resorts distributed around the new state in or near former centres of cultural and social life in pre-Mandate Palestine. They could use their time allocation in one trip or make two or more trips. They could also extend their trips by paying a modest additional cost. Air fares would be covered for two trips a year.

Every Palestinian would be able to choose such a resort within, say, 15 kilometres of his or her former home town or village. I calculate that much of the inhabited areas of the new state could be covered by about 100 such communities. They could be repositories of local culture and history, telling of the local area as it was in pre-Mandate Palestine.

It seems to me that these options – compensation, and rehousing or timesharing – will provide satisfaction to most Palestinians outside Israel, but there are also 1.4 million Palestinian Arabs inside Israel who have chafed under the hostility, lies, aggression and discrimination of successive Israeli governments, starting with the harsh military administration I mentioned earlier.

Of course, they would automatically become citizens of the new state, but they should also be entitled to some financial compensation for decades of suffering and deprivation, long with 'timeshare' privileges if they are now living away from their original homes.

They might be ideal people to be paid for some kind of 'greeting and consultation' role in the nearest resort to their home village.

Takeup

It is difficult to be very precise, but we could make a guess at the numbers of Palestinians who would take up each option.

Considering the various groups above, here is an estimate of how many might take each option. Bear in mind that all Palestinians will be able to take up the "timeshare" option, but only some will avail themselves of it. My guesstimates therefore relate to the likely annual uptake.

Middle East refugees in camps (4.5 million): Timeshare 15% (675,000); permanent return 75% (3,375,000) (In each group there will be some who are content to take just the generous compensation on offer.)

Middle East refugees in established homes/jobs (4 million): Timeshare 25% (1 million); permanent return 45% (1,800,000)

"Diaspora" Palestinians (4 million): Timeshare 50% (1,600,000); permanent return 20% (800,000)

So the total expected to return permanently on these estimates is about six million. This is still a large number, but the largest proportion is people who have lived statelessly and deprived for seventy years, and if anyone should return to a homeland they left unwillingly, it is them.

But where would they all go, people sometimes say? Could tiny little Israel accommodate all those extra people. (Of course, it wouldn't be Israel any more, and it wouldn't be quite as tiny.)

If you doubled the population of the new state there would still be 1000 square metres for every inhabitant. Of course, as an average this doesn't mean very much, but Israel at the moment has a population density of 371 people per square kilometer. It is number 32 in the world rankings of population density. There are 17 countries at the top of the list with more than double that density; and 7 with more than four times. Admittedly many of these are city states but nevertheless, there is a long way to go before the new state would be overcrowded. Anyone who has been to Israel and Palestine knows that there are large areas away from the coastal belt in which new towns or additions to existing towns could be built and still leave plenty of breathing space. A lot of the area of Israel is the Negev desert, but there are already plans for new towns in those areas. Admittedly, as a destination for returning Palestinians it would not be attractive, apart from those few whose families came from that area.

Salman Abu Sitta and his Palestine Land Society have done more than anyone else to map Palestine and gather demographic statistics. He points out that Gaza has a population density of 7000 people per square kilometre, while the areas outside Gaza in the northern Negev, from which many of the refugees came, has a population density of 7 per square kilometre. His maps show that it would be easy for all those refugees living in Gaza to return to their homes without disruption to the existing Jewish population who live in that sparsely populated area.

The Palestine Land Society has prepared maps which show that most Jews in Israel live outside areas to which Palestinians would choose to return. This may sound surprising but many villages were destroyed and their sites abandoned. They are now in the middle of agricultural areas, national parks or undeveloped land. While it might have been attractive for the new Israelis to take over existing Arab houses and even whole towns in 1948, building an Israeli community on the site of a ruined village would be unnecessarily complicated when there was so much virgin land available.

Even in the area around Tel Aviv with the largest concentration of Jews, and with the largest areas of land owned by Jews before 1948, the PLS maps show that most built-up areas are not on previously Arab-owned land. Or to put it another way, the return of Palestinian Arabs to their villages even in the Tel Aviv area would not involve displacing many Jews, which would be voluntary anyway. Indeed, there might be some former Israeli Jews who would actually enjoy living in what would become mixed Jewish-Arab communities. Jaffa today is a little like that.

In the new state there would be a large increase in architecture, construction, roadbuilding, education, healthcare and the commercial activities needed to supply the new – and newly prosperous – inhabitants. But of course, among the returners would be architects, construction experts, engineers, doctors, teachers and so on. And the compensation would not just sit in their pockets but be spent in the new state and contribute to its prosperity.

Even the Palestinians who stayed at home and didn't opt for a full return or the timeshare option, might still chose to visit their homeland, using their new passports and spending money in the new state on their trips.

And if someone says water supply is a problem, consider this: at the moment Israel sells West Bankers their own water, and restricts their supply to a fifth of the total, the rest going to Israel and the settlements. A fairer sharing of water plus a major effort to increase desalination could overcome many problems.

Before I return to more general arguments, I want to say one further thing about this whirlwind – and possibly mind-bending – tour of possible options and their costs. If you think that the plan for the right of return described above is totally unrealistic, infeasible and unaffordable this should have nothing to do with your acceptance of the fact that something has to be done to redress the loss of rights experienced by Palestinians.

Establishing a Right of Return for Palestinians does not depend on how much it will cost. It is their right, whatever it costs. Israel over the years has instituted a right of return for any Jew in the world (as well as anyone with at least one Jewish grandparent) meaning that theoretically 23 million people could turn up on its doorstep and claim citizenship[14]. No one has sat down and done the sums about what that 'return' would cost. It is seen as an absolute right and in the unlikely event that all 23 million turned up, Israel would feel committed to honour its promise. Of course, in spite of Israel describing itself as the state of all Jews, barely a third of the world's Jews seem to want to travel to it and live there. Perhaps for them the whole idea of 'returning' to a place you have never been to and with which you have no connection other than a sentimental one, is seen for the nonsense it is.

[14] DellaPergola, Sergio (2015). Dashefsky, Arnold; Sheskin, Ira, eds. "World Jewish Population, 2015". Current Jewish Population Reports. The American Jewish Year Book (Dordrecht: Springer). 115: 273–364. Retrieved 19 November 2016.

9   The new state

We can now combine the two ideas I have suggested to ask a question whose answer depends on the interaction between both ideas – the single state and the right of return for Palestinians. That question is: What will it be like, this new state?

The answer is fundamentally different from how you might describe the entity or entities that could come into existence as a result of a Two-State Solution, or even a Federal State of Israel and Palestine. Both of these would involve a very different interpretation of the Right of Return, since Israel as it exists today would be one partner in the negotiations, and any idea of Palestinians returning to what is now Israel has been rejected out of hand. (So much for negotiating without preconditions).

There is a book called *The Palestinian Refugee Problem: The Search for a Solution*[15], and while its ideas are very helpful in formulating mechanisms

---

[15] The Palestinian Refugee Problem: *The Search for a Solution*, Edited by Rex Brynen and Roula El-Rifai, Pluto Press, 2014

by which the huge task could be tackled, it is based on the idea that the solution will emerge as a result of negotiations between Israel and Palestine, with the participation of other nations and organisations. But as I've tried to suggest above, negotiating with any Israeli government which is determined to hold on to its existing territory and continue to define itself as a Jewish state will produce no solution at all which is acceptable to the Palestinians. The occasional Israeli references to the right of return in previous peace negotiations have been laughable. The idea that only 25,000 of the millions with a right to return to what is now Israel should be permitted to return is little more than a cruel joke. There is no just alternative to a right of return for Palestinians to all of pre-Mandate Palestine. Attempts to find such alternatives are as doomed as the search for perpetual motion.

In considering how this solution to the Palestine-Israel problem might come about, we have to look at two processes which will probably happen in parallel. There is the transformation of the old entities of Israel and the West Bank and Gaza into the new state, and the planning and instigation of the programme of return.

The setting up of the new state would start with the dismantling and reassembling the machinery of statecraft. A constitution would be devised, elections held throughout the territory, international guarantees organised, and amalgamation of infrastructures initiated. In some ways, it would be like the reunification of Germany. The whole area between the Jordan and the Mediterranean was one state that became split into two and now has to be reassembled, just like East and West Germany. Everything should be done to reduce or eliminate a proprietorial attitude among the different affiliations which will have joined together in one state. No one should object if, say, the "Jewish" parliament building, the Knesset, was turned into the parliament for the new state. It would no longer be Jewish, just as Bir Zeit University, say, would no longer be Arab.

There would be a major reassessment of international relations, now that the new state was no longer a pariah state with one or two international supporters. New trade deals, both with Arab countries and the rest of the world, would need to be negotiated, the educational system reorganised so that schools and universities would be open to anyone and new syllabuses written. The tourist industry would be a major priority, with an increase in numbers of visitors, no longer worried by security issues, and able now to visit all areas for as long as they like, rather than being rushed in and out of Bethlehem in an hour by Israeli tour agents, so that they don't buy souvenirs or food from Arab establishments. There would probably be a need for a second airport, perhaps near Ramallah. (There was one once at Kalandia, now a notorious checkpoint.)

As I mentioned earlier, the settlements would no longer be an issue in a new state, although the settlers might be, if they don't accept the new situation. Security systems would have to be dismantled, apartheid roads would now be available to all, and there would have to be a rationalisation of the two-tier roads system on the West Bank. While no settler would be removed from his house, those who live in the settlements would have to accept that when a house becomes empty, its new tenants could be from any religion or none, not just Jews.

At the same time, there would be the process of setting up the Office of Palestinian Return, assembling its budget, assessing the wishes of Palestinians, planning the huge construction programme, setting up a Ministry of Return to the new state, surveying the land for the hundred 'resorts', developing the existing excellent survey by the Palestine Land Society of destroyed villages to begin to plan reconstruction or new housebuilding, and laying out new roads to ensure that travel between the now reunited areas will be efficient.

Many of these plans can be made before the full details are available of what option different Palestinians will choose. The total cost can be estimated and spending begin before refugees' choices have been finalised. There already exist designs for a number of destroyed villages, as part of a competition by the Palestine Land Society. (See Appendix 3) There is even a database for many villages, containing details of which families lived there and in which houses.

The money involved will fuel a construction boom. If planned properly it can make use of the talents and skills of returning Palestinians who might be identified early on and work on a consultancy basis to carry out the huge number of tasks. It will also provide a boost in employment for Palestinians who live in poverty on the West Bank and in Gaza, and have been cut off from working in Israel.

What are the likely causes of friction in this new state? Why would the Jewish inhabitants be hostile to the Arabs, both 'old' citizens and new ones?

Well, I can't rule out one new factor, and that could be jealousy and animosity felt by Jews, particularly poorer ones, towards the Palestinian Arabs who turn up from the West Bank and Gaza, or further afield, with their wallets bulging with compensation money, moving into brand new or nicely renovated houses, with new furniture and fittings, and an annual income, all at the state's expense. Only, of course, it wouldn't be only at the new state's expense. The funding of this programme would have to come from a wide range of organisations and aid agencies, and this would be money in the state's exchequer which would not be there if there wasn't a return programme. There is also the fact that one aim of the new state would be to even out the disparities of rich and poor, and many poor Jews as well as poor Palestinians would benefit from this.

One other factor to point out is that, in addition to the funds being restitution for the pain and loss the Palestinians have suffered, they are also some kind of replacement of what Israel and Israelis stole from them in 1948. During the six weeks before Israel was declared a state on 14 May, and while the British Mandate was still in force, Jewish forces attacked and depopulated 220 Palestinian villages, creating half of the total refugee population today. In these attacks a score or more of massacres and atrocities were committed, the most notorious of which was the Deir Yassin massacre carried out on 9 April 1948. And when Palestinians left or were pushed out of their homes, some homes were destroyed but the better ones were often taken over by Israelis who appropriated the contents, often including valuables and money, as if they had a natural right to do so. There are touching stories by Palestinians who have visited Israel from abroad and called on the current tenants of the houses they used to live in. Apart from facing the almost inevitable rejection of a request to see inside, such visitors have told of glimpsing a valuable piano, carpets, pictures and family possessions, all stolen directly or indirectly by the current inhabitants or their predecessors.

Widely documented as this campaign of destruction and theft is, Israel has never admitted responsibility for it, but in any discussion about who should pay for the right of return we can be sure that Israel, or whoever tries to look after its interests in the new state, will kick and scream when funds are allocated to the return programme.

The benefits accruing to the state and its citizens after 1948, not least the 94% of the Jewish partition area which was not owned by Jews before 1948, were considerable and it is only right that that should be taken into account when considering any good fortune they might appear now to be benefitting from.

But a more obvious potential source of friction in the new state is a continuation of the hostility and aggression that has marked the last seventy years between Israelis and Palestinians. I can only offer some reasons why I think this will not occur although for many others, such friction is their main reason for thinking that One Democratic State will not happen.

First, the Jewish inhabitants of the new state: what will their grievance be against the Muslims or Christians who are now equal citizens? Currently, hostility to Palestinians among some Israelis takes various forms.

There is frank racism, for example, typified by the 'Arabs never hug their children' remark. There's nothing we can do about that except to pass strict laws outlawing anti-Arab racism along with anti-semitism, and banning all discrimination in the new state on grounds of race or religion.

Then, there is the association in the minds of some Jews of all Palestinian citizens of the new state with past episodes of terrorism. This, like frank racism, is unjust. But there will be Palestinian citizens of the new state who are self-acknowledged militants, associated over the years with protests against Israeli occupation, settler violence, and the destruction of Gaza. But since the reasons for their militancy will have been removed, it is unlikely that there will be a continuing anti-Zionist movement, if we can call it that, because the Zionist entity of Israel will no longer be in control of Arabs' lives. Jews in the new state might be justified in objecting to the fact that they are no longer in a majority, or are even in a minority, but such objections, to be legitimate, would have to be based on actual discrimination or deprivation.

It is true that there may be citizens of the new state who have actually committed violence against Israel, either directly, through attacking soldiers or settlers, or indirectly, through launching rockets into formerly Israeli territory. Clearly some kind of amnesty would have to operate such that when Israeli security files are transferred to the new government, there isn't a continuation of the hunting down and illegal assassination of alleged terrorists.

But if such an amnesty is also applied to the many more perpetrators of Israeli violence against innocent Arabs, it will be seen that on balance, the Jewish citizens of the new state will have less cause for harbouring grudges against former Arab resistance fighters than the Arabs will against Jewish soldiers and settlers, as well as politicians who have fomented anti-Arab violence over the years.

There is also the fear that has motivated Israel in the past and led to its huge military budget (with the side benefit of a large and profitable defence industry) – that it is vulnerable to attack from Arab countries.

Clearly, as long as Israel suppresses and commits war crimes against an Arab people, it will be a potential target for Arab regimes elsewhere in the Middle East and will be able to rely on the security argument to terrify its citizens. But, as

Virginia Tilley points out in her book *The One-State Solution:*

> The logic [of the security argument] is ... circular in arguing that Jewish statehood is essential to protect Jews from the consequences of Jewish statehood. For the awkward fact is that, if Palestinians came to enjoy democratic rights as citizens in one secular-democratic state, the threat of Arab attack would disappear entirely, as Arab states would have no motive to attack such a state.[16]

There will no doubt be a rearguard action either by religious Jews or rightwing settlers, or both, against the perceived loss of the 'Jewishness' of the state. But what will that actually mean in real terms? One of the key elements in the constitution of the new state will be clauses which protect freedom of religious practice for all creeds, as well as the freedom not to adhere to any religion. The life of a Jewish citizen of the new state will not be changed one whit by having to share citizenship with a large number of Muslim, Christian, or atheist Palestinians.

There may be a need to find ways in which Jews are able to avoid the affront of cultural practice, clothing, different dietary rules and so on, but these are common to all societies in which observant Jews live and ways are usually found to allow them to practice their religion without being interfered with – or interfering with – people of other faiths or no faiths. It is true that the Palestinians in the new state will now not be discriminated against in the way that Israeli Palestinians are today. They will have facilities for health, education, roads, justice, and parliamentary representation which are comparable with, rather than inferior to, those experienced by many Jews today in Israel. But I cannot see how sharing the state fairly will disadvantage any of the

---

[16] The One-State Solution, Virginia Tilley.

Jewish inhabitants of the new state.

There is undoubtedly an important symbolism for some Jews, many outside Palestine, in there being a "Jewish state" somewhere in the world (in which, as I have remarked most Jews do not want to live). The value of this symbolism, presumably, lies in the belief that one day, perhaps, a resurgence of anti-semitism will make life for Jews living outside Palestine intolerable and without a Jewish state there will be nowhere for them to go.

There are two answers to this. One is that this is an exaggerated belief created by Israel and its supporters. We have seen recently in the UK figures purporting to show an increase in anti-semitism, released by organisations which claim to monitor such incidents. One recent newspaper headline 'Prevalence of hate speech 'shocking…' [17] turns out to be based on an increase in the number of people "who have witnessed hate speech in the past year." This is a pretty tenuous piece of evidence for an increase in hate speech. If the organisation had given figures for people who had been the target of hate speech the evidence might have been a little less tendentious. But the number of witnesses to an event has little evidential value when trying to assess the number of events. But my second answer to people who harbour the fear that one day they might need a place of refuge that could only be supplied by a Jewish state is that the chances of the sort of virulent state-sanctioned racism that led to the destruction of European Jews is so minuscule that it is not a valid reason for supporting the existence of a state – the Jewish state of Israel – which is itself racist in conception and execution.

There is a potential safeguard, which I offer hesitantly. It might not be supported by many Palestinians who feel that the world has gone far enough in accommodating the sensitivities of Jews who do not live in Israel but nevertheless fear that one day they might have to. But it could be the case that,

---

[17] *The Guardian*, 27th January, 2018

although the law of return for Jews, particularly the 23 million people who have at least one Jewish grandparent, would not form part of the new state, I could conceive of some sort of immigration law that would, under certain circumstances, allow privileged status to some Jews. They would have to make a case in order to fit a set of qualifications, which might relate to evidence of genuine persecution, such as many countries apply to asylum seekers. There might also be special privileges for Jews, and there are some, who precisely because of the racist and criminal behaviour of past Israeli governments have refused to live there even though they have a family connection with Palestine.

In my view, there will be no justification for hostility by Jewish members of the new state towards its Palestinian Arab citizens. This doesn't mean it won't occur, but with a rigorous set of anti-discrimination laws and a strong, well-organised law enforcement system, I think any hostility can be contained.

Now, for the possibility of anti-Jew hostility among Arabs. It is interesting that this suggestion is most often put forward by supporters of Israel. To a certain extent, it is a product of the myth fostered by Zionists and successive Israeli governments, either explicitly or implicitly, that all Palestinians are anti-semitic. This is partly a result of the way in which in the Mandate period the threat to Palestinian Arabs was spoken of and written about as coming from 'the Jews.' Many Palestinian Arabs, as they saw the increasing hold that Zionists had over the British government, through daily access to senior politicians in Whitehall, and the dominating presence of the Jewish Agency in Palestine, inevitably spoke about 'the enemy' as *Jews*, adopting the Zionists' own terms. The megaphone diplomacy of the Zionists was always in terms of *Jews* – to create a *Jewish* state, to bring the *Jews* of the world to Palestine, to increase *Jewish* immigration, to increase the representation of *Jews* in the government. Because of this, the Arabs can hardly be blamed for directing their hostility towards Jews, but this is no more anti-semitic than Cold War fears of Russia and what the 'Russians' did were anti-slav.

When violence was directed by Arabs in Palestine at Jews, before or after 1948, it was not analogous to the violence of Nazis against Jews but to the violence of the French Resistance against Germans.

In the new state, while former Israelis as individuals might be seen as having supported the oppression of Palestinians, it is unlikely that the Jews as a group will be threatened or need protection against the returning Palestinian Arabs. Jews are not attacked by the Arabs who live in Israel today – why should that change in the new state? In any case, as with the possibility of anti-Arab racism, strong laws and law enforcement should be able to deal with the situation.

Before I seem impossibly starry-eyed, I am not saying there will be no crime in the new state. Of course, there is the possibility of formerly Israeli thugs attacking Arab immigrants, or indeed former members of Islamic Jihad clinging to old habits. But these – if they occur – will be treated as criminals committing crimes, not as existential threats to the state.

10 Biting the bullet

By now, even readers who accept the justice of the argument for a right of return for Palestinians to a single democratic state may be quailing at the likely costs of such a scheme. Six-figure compensation amounts for 12 million people, hundreds of destroyed villages rebuilt, existing ones expanded, and entirely new towns and villages designed and built, a hundred 'resorts' designed and constructed the entire length of the land, and of course an entire bureaucracy set up in Palestine and abroad to handle the huge scheme.

Let's now look at some costs. I'm afraid I am going to treat this like a Fermi question, rather than hire a team of quantity surveyors, international aid experts, chartered accountants and demographers. What is a Fermi question?[18] Well, it's a way of answering questions in science where you don't know much about the topic. It relies on guesswork and hunch but, done properly, it can come up

[18] *The Hair of the Dog*, Karl Sabbagh, John Murray, 2010

with answers which are sometimes only several times – or a fraction of – the correct answer which would be obtained after months of detailed analysis. This may not sound very impressive but scientists are happy when they are within an order of magnitude (ten times or a tenth) of the correct answer.

Enrico Fermi was an Italian-American physicist who worked on the atomic bomb. He estimated the strength of the atomic bomb that detonated at the Trinity test, based on the distance travelled by pieces of paper he dropped from his hand during the blast. His estimate of 10 kilotons of TNT was remarkably close to the now-accepted value of around 20 kilotons. He used to teach the method he had used by asking students in his classes to work out how many piano tuners there were in Chicago, using just their own very limited knowledge.

So, it is Fermi time – first, the capital investment needed to set up the houses and resorts. (I have made slightly different assumptions from those of the Palestine Land Society which has assumed 5 residents per house or flat. I have assumed slightly fewer.)

With six million Palestinians, say, returning, to 1,500,000 new housing units, flats or houses, in 516 destroyed villages, the total cost of construction has been worked out at about $60 billion[19]. A housing unit could be a single-occupancy house or a two-apartment building. This is less than $12,000 per head. It sounds low but it is based on an average occupancy of four people per unit. I suspect that is too high for some. There will be elderly couples who want a place of their own, or younger couples with one or two children. But it is a useful benchmark. That $60 billion compares favourably with how much Israel has spent over the years building settlements and the necessary apartheid roads to reach them. For 500,000 settlers Israel has spent $17 billion, about $34,000 per head.

In addition to the new villages, there will be some Palestinians moving into existing houses in villages or towns,

---

[19] Figures from Palestine Land Society, http://www.plands.org/en/home

which have been vacated by Jews, perhaps settlers, who might not want to stay, as well as the renovation of existing unused or derelict housing. The so-called Arab quarter of my father's home town, Safad, is a run-down jumble of derelict houses, gift shops, 'art' galleries and empty sites. The whole area could be renovated for much less than the cost of building all new houses.

These amounts are of the same order of magnitude as is Israel's defence budget over about three years. Israel spends on defence $16-18bn a year, much of it with money provided by the US. The US has given Israel $40 billion since 2000, and has promised $38 billion over the next ten years. A commitment to a similar amount over the next ten years, from the exchequer of the new state, with matching amounts from other UN members, including the rich Arab countries, and a diversion of the state's own budget from security, settlement building, religious subsidies and so on would provide the sort of money that will be needed for the massive new building programme.

The timeshare option is slightly more difficult to price, and there are various factors which might mitigate the costs.

I am suggesting a hundred resorts. How many people/ nights would they have to accommodate? Let's say, Fermi-style, that 2,825,000 people would each be entitled to stay 14 nights. Let's assume an average of 2.5 people per room. So the number of rooms needed for those two weeks would be 1,130,000 – if they all stayed at the same time. But if they were spread over a year, the number of rooms needed would be 47,000. If these were divided among, say, 100 resorts each would have to have 470 rooms. These would not be boutique hotels but nor would they be Las Vegas behemoths with 6000 rooms. At $50 million per resort, say, that would total $5 billion capital costs.

Associated with the rehousing option and the timeshare option there would be annual costs. In the case of those who return permanently, I suggest an annual income of, say, $10,000 per family, and utilities costs of, say, $2,000. So $12,000 p.a. for three million homesteads comes to $36 billion p.a. In the case of the timeshare, there would be the maintenance, food provision, staffing and so on. Let's say $50 per room per day. That comes to about $8 million per resort, so a total of $800 million p.a.

So the two types of returners – the permanent residents and the visitors, would require a capital investment of about £120 billion over ten years and an annual outlay of, say, £40 billion.

Now the biggest imponderable is the compensation, to which everyone would be entitled. I'm sure there will be much discussion over issues like: should every Palestinian – pre – 1948ers and their children and grandchildren – be entitled to the same amount? I think the comparatively small number of survivors from the mandate period should be entitled to more than the rest. It is pretty easy to work out who they are, and they are likely to have suffered most, even if they were babies at the time of the Nakba. In terms of numbers, there are unlikely to be more than 2% of the total, say 250,000.

If the amounts for that 2% were, say, twice or three times what the rest received that would not make much difference to the total, so let's say $50,000 per Palestinian and see where that gets us. $600 billion dollars in compensation. Hmm. Add that to the money for rebuilding houses and new construction of villages and resorts and you get a grand total of about $720 billion. Fermi-style, this could be as much as a trillion dollars ($1,000,000,000,000).

There are of course other costs involved. The salaries and administration costs of the actual programme that would have to be set up to make all this happen are incalculable. One issue which is often forgotten in considering the costs of a right of return is compensation due to the host countries, principally Lebanon, Syria and Jordan. Over the seventy years of the conflict, these states have devoted a lot of resources to hosting Palestinian refugees. (Not always ungrudgingly, it has to be said.) It is not easy to calculate exact amounts but it cannot be denied that without Israel's creation of the refugee problem those states would not have had to host dispossessed people in their millions. Once a viable programme for return of refugees is under way, the host countries will quite rightly demand that their costs be recognised. But it is also the case that the host countries will benefit from compensation payments to those refugees who choose to stay where they are. A Palestinian living a successful and settled life in Amman or Beirut with his family may choose to stay where he is, and the compensation he receives will then be spent or invested in the host country.

In considering these large amounts, I would say that if something is required by natural justice or law, then its cost must be met. Germany accepted the payment of thousands of dollars in reparations to each survivor of the Nazi holocaust, even though it is no longer a Nazi state and most of its citizens today view the Holocaust with horror. How much greater is Israel's responsibility when it continues to deny that the Palestinian Arabs were dispossessed by its own deliberate actions and when there are still Israelis alive today who were the perpetrators of that dispossession? Of course, I am talking about a future in which Israel as it is today does not exist, but the new state will take over the assets and obligations of Israel and will have resources to contribute to a right of return programme. Israel has a GDP of about $380 billion and even just diverting security savings towards setting up the new state and bringing home the refugees will make a significant contribution. It has been calculated that the cost to Israel of its voluntary occupation of the West Bank and Gaza since the Oslo talks is about $260 billion. Such costs would no longer be necessary in the new state.

But there are other, hidden, sources of funding. One element in the figure for losses due to the occupation is the decline in tourism, with an estimate loss of over $40 billion, as a result of fears of violence, and tight Israeli control of many of the sites in Palestinian areas. Not only would that $40 billion be available to the new state, but a revived, comprehensive and well-publicised tourism campaign could double or treble it. Visitors will be able to come to the new state and see all the major Roman, Byzantine, Muslim, and Christian sites in a couple of days, instead of the cumbersome arrangements that apply at present where many visitors to Israel never visit the

West Bank and Gaza because of the all-pervasive checkpoints and the fabricated fears of terrorism. Today's visitors from abroad rarely go into significant Arab towns like Nazareth, Jaffa or Acre because their Israeli travel guides concentrate on Jewish sites. With the state no longer being exclusively Jewish there will be an upsurge of archaeological discoveries. As Nadia Abu el-Haj points out in her book *Facts on the Ground*, archaeology in Israel has concentrated exclusively on establishing a Jewish presence in the area, ignoring and often destroying evidence of other civilizations or ethnic group:

> The most controversial practice in Israeli archaeology has been the use of bulldozers on archaeological sites. ... [B]ulldozers are used in order to get down to the earlier strata, which are saturated with national significance, as quickly as possible (Iron Age through early-Roman). During the excavation of the biblical site of Jezreel in which I participated, a bulldozer was used in order to more quickly determine the direction and structure of the Iron Age moat. .... At both the Jezreel excavations and the Jerusalem excavations, archaeologists moved through dirt rather quickly. Israeli excavators tend to use large shovels, pickaxes, and large buckets in order to move through the earth. In contrast, for example, the European (mostly British) trained archaeologists at Jezreel explained that they would prefer to excavate with smaller tools and slower digging techniques, including, for example, sifting dirt in search of very small remains: artifactual, animal, seeds, and so forth.[20]

In excavating in search of Herodian and Judaic remains, the Israeli archaeologist Yigael Yadin wanted to destroy remains of the Umayyad Islamic period to get beneath them for more evidence of Jewish history. He was unconcerned about any other cultures who also had a presence in Palestine, and the

---

[20] Nadia Abu El-Haj, *Facts on the Ground*, University of Chicago Press, 2001, p. 148

destruction was only prevented by another Israeli archaeologist with a less chauvinistic view of his task. There was a general devil-may-care attitude to scholarship in the early years of Israel's existence. Moshe Dayan, one-eyed minister of defence, was fond of stealing important artifacts to display in his home and garden. Yadin is quoted as saying of one valuable piece which had gone missing: "I know who did it, and I am not going to say who it is, but if I catch him, I'll poke out his other eye, too."

Since, in fact, the Jews in Palestine were only one of a number of important and interesting cultural groups, a less biased and – I might say – more professional approach to archaeology in the new state could be a potent source of new discoveries, generating a large increase in tourism.

There is another potential source of visitor revenue in the new state. The influx of Palestinians returning to their roots would bring new income, even though their travel and accommodation costs would be covered by the Right of Return scheme. Some of the Right of Return budget will end up back in the hands of the new state, through wages for construction workers, hotel service workers, and others who will be needed to cope with the influx.

The Boycott, Divestment and Sanctions campaign has been having a significant effect on such visitors as academics who have been reluctant to link up with Israeli universities, and entertainers who have avoided Israel because of its policies towards the Palestinians. These will now be more willing to visit and by doing so they will draw attention in the rest of the world to the pluralistic democracy that has arrived in the Middle East. And the entertainers will attract more visitors, perhaps from neighbouring Arab countries to attend their performances. There is also likely to be a general increase in visitors from neighbouring countries, the Gulf and Saudi Arabia, bringing revenue to the luxury end of the tourism market.

The points above have really just scratched the surface of how the costs of a properly funded right of return programme will not be all negative. But there will be a need for a concerted effort to raise money among a whole range of local and international bodies in order to get the right of return scheme off to a good start. There would be nothing worse than a huge fanfare over the creation of a single state between the Jordan and the Mediterranean, accompanied by promises of compensation and the right to return to their homes, followed by years of inactivity and continuing Palestinian deprivation. Inevitably there will be Palestinians who hear the news they have longed to hear for 70 years but who will die before such a scheme is in place.

However you look at it, $720 billion is a lot of money. However else you look at it, it is what the Palestinians are owed. And this is not like the situation where you owe the tax man a lot of money and he agrees a negotiated reduction. The Palestinians have suffered enough. They will have no interest in accepting less than they deserve. And indeed, I don't know whether the hypothetical amounts I have suggested will be acceptable. I initially had in mind a figure of a million dollars per refugee. After all, $14,000 p.a. compensation for 70 years of deprivation does not seem unreasonable. My suggestion of $100,000 for the oldest is a paltry $1,400 per year of loss. Seen in that light it is far from generous or extravagant.

We need to understand why so much money is necessary. The Israelis expelled 750,000 Palestinians. If they had stayed, they would still be 12 million by now. But they and their families would have had 70 years of living in a beautiful, historic country, intermarrying, studying, getting good jobs, swimming in the Mediterranean, travelling and returning home, electing their own MPs and governments, not having lies told about them as 'terrorists', and, above all, having a national identity of which they could be proud. This 12 million would not have seen, or heard stories of, the murders, assassinations, imprisonments, and brutalisation of their relatives; they would not have watched news of several wars on television where their enemy invented excuses for taking over more Palestinian land, fabricated stories to the news media about being under existential threat, or hurled accusations of anti-semitism against anybody who criticised these actions.

However it is raised, the world should not begrudge spending money on the solution to a problem which has been a running sore for the last seventy years and in hidden costs has incurred far more than $720 billion. It is not too fanciful to say that several major wars would not have happened if Palestine had been given its independence as a single democratic state in 1948. Wars like the Iraq war were not fought over Palestine, but underlying the causes of that Middle East war and others was the perception of the West – and particularly America – as supporters and funders of a settler colonial enterprise in the heart of the Arab world. How could the Arabs trust a country which they knew to be lying on behalf of its client state, funding it to the hilt, and quashing any attempt to present the truth about what Israel has done to the Palestinians?

The Iraq War has cost about two trillion dollars [21] ($2,000,000,000,000). All America's wars in the Middle East probably cost $5 trillion. Suppose the creation of the new state and the removal of the major source of friction and distrust in the Middle East reduced future wars by, say, 20%. That would mean that for a cost of $720 billion the world saved a trillion dollars, a net profit of $280 billion. And if wars in the Middle East were halved as a result of the new world order created by the new state, the world would be better off by nearly two trillion dollars.

[21] https://www.reuters.com/article/us-iraq-war-anniversary/iraq-war-costs-u-s-more-than-2-trillion-study-idUSBRE92D0PG20130314

11   A scenario

By this stage in the book, you may be wondering to yourself "what is this man smoking?" So much of what I'm suggesting seems far beyond the realms of possibility against a daily background of conflict, aggression, inhumanity and terrorism, which most people interpret as an inevitable consequence of age-old animosities between Arab and Jew.

But I believe that it has been in Israel's interest to create a picture of its oppression of the Palestinians as a response to Palestinian actions rather than as what it actually is – a decades-long attempt to get rid of them, so that Israel can be the genuinely Jewish state some Jews want it to be.

That is, a state which is 'racially' pure (even though the Jews are not a race), and which is allowed to act only in its own interests on the world stage, requiring special treatment from the rest of the world as some kind of recompense for the persecution of Jews over the centuries. In other words, an anachronism in the modern world.

But in fact, many Jews, particularly those outside Israel but plenty inside too, do not see their place in the world in that way. Among themselves, and in internet groups like *J Street* and *Jews for Justice for Palestinians*, many Jews would welcome a state in Palestine that is actually democratic and accepts responsibility for the harm Israel and Zionism has done to Palestinians in the past. There are actually many 'One-Staters' among these Jews, who support the idea of sharing the entire territory between the Jordan and the Mediterranean, who have Palestinian friends, and who believe that each group has much to give the other, culturally and politically.

So to address the elephant in the room – how could One Democratic State, with the right of return for Palestinians, possibly come about?

I'd like to paint one scenario of many, based on the 'butterfly wing' theory of historical contingency.

Like many major shifts in international politics, it depends on the simultaneous occurrence of several events, often in themselves quite trivial, which tip the situation into an entirely new set of circumstances.

Here are some eventualities, where a combination of some or all of them could shift the opinions of Israelis, other Jews, and the world outside towards the realisation that one single state for Jews and Palestinians is the only way to avoid another seventy years of brutal conflict:

- **A succession of outrageous actions by Israel against the Palestinians.**

These would be accompanied by the usual fabricated reasons why such actions are necessary to preserve the security of the state. This at least is not just possible but a regular feature of the Israel-Palestine conflict.

As I write, Israel's imprisonment of 16-year-old Ahed Tamimi is demonstrating its usual inability to look beyond its hatred of Palestinians, and in particular, their temerity to resist its illegal occupation.

There are many Jews who are made uncomfortable by such actions, even including former members of the Shin Beth, Israel's security organisation, who spoke out in the documentary The Gatekeepers.

- **A political/social scandal, worse than the usual ones.**

One reason Israel ignores international law and the criticisms of many countries and world organisations is that its government over the years has contained a high proportion of rather unpleasant people. Two of its prime ministers in its first four decades were former terrorists in the Mandate years, with a list of assassinations and bombings to their debit, who justified terrorism to obtain Zionist objectives.

One of them, Yitzhak Shamir, is quoted as saying in public that "it is permissible to lie for the sake of the Land of Israel," so it is not unreasonable to discount official Israel explanations for its actions.

The other terrorist PM, Menachem Begin, described Palestinians as "beasts walking on two legs" and said that "if Hitler was sitting in a house with 20 other people, wouldn't it be correct to blow up the house?

Recently, as a result of a huge influx of right wing Russian emigrés, not all of them Jewish, and their acquisition of political power through forming shaky coalitions, there is a breed of Israeli politician who is not afraid to say in public what others only say in private.

One of them, foreign minister Avigdor Lieberman, with a conviction for assault, said in 2015 that Israeli Arabs who are disloyal to Israel should be beheaded, taking a leaf from ISIS, perhaps. These are not nice people, and some of them have been the subject of criminal investigations.

Indeed, the roll call of Israeli politicians actually convicted of crimes is a long one:

President Moshe Katsav – rape and obstruction of justice
Prime Minister Ehud Olmert – breach of trust and bribery
Aharon Abuhatzira, Minister of Religious Services (sic)
– larceny, breach of trust, and fraud
Shlomo Benizri, Minister of Health and Labor and Social Welfare -- bribes, breach of faith, obstructing justice, etc
Aryeh Deri, Minister of Internal Affairs – bribes

Tzachi Hanegbi, Minister of Justice, Minister of Internal Security, and Minister of Intelligence and Nuclear Affairs – perjury and moral turpitude

Avraham Hirschson, Israeli Minister of Finance – theft of 2 million shekels

Yitzhak Mordechai, Israel's Minister of Defense and Minister of Transport – harassment

Rafael Pinhasi, Minister of Communications – illegal transfer of funds

Haim Ramon, Israel's Minister of Health, Minister of Internal Affairs, and Minister of Justice – assault

Gonen Segev, National Infrastructure Minister – drug smuggling, forgery and fraud[22]

An equal number of members of the Israeli parliament, past and present, also have criminal records.

At the time of writing, the current Israeli prime minister has been questioned by police on at least five occasions over the last few months in connection with possible corruption charges.

I am pointing this out not so much to condemn the morals of Israeli politicians and members of parliament – no one is perfect – but to suggest that the scope is there for a really major scandal that might finally alienate Jewish support in Israel and abroad for the current Israeli government and prompt support for a clean sweep of government that might result in a surprise election outcome.

- **Revival of the peace movement.**

There is a small but active peace movement in Israel, including many people who support the idea of a single state, which could make a splash with a major demonstration criticising the absence of any moves for peace by Israel,

---

[22] https://en.wikipedia.org/wiki/List_of_Israeli_public_officials_convicted_of_crimes_or_misdemeanors

suddenly revealing to the world that not all Israelis have the same hostility to a peace agreement. It's worth noting, on the wider stage, that support for a Jewish state among Jews outside Israel is also waning. Among younger U.S. Jews, aged 18-34 – the decision-makers of the future – only 40% are comfortable with the idea of a Jewish state. And only 30% sympathise more with Israel than with Palestine in the Arab-Israeli conflict.[23]

- **A new push for peace by Palestinian politicians.**

It's sad to have to say this but, in spite of incessant Israeli claims to the contrary, there has always been a partner for peace in Palestine. But it has to be a just peace, and the Israelis have never come within a million miles of offering one, deliberately. Because Israel does not want any accommodation with a people some of its citizens still believe to be 'beasts on two legs. The Palestinians have often been described as the 'victims of the victims' and it is difficult to understand why the atrocities committed on Jews by a European nation have been cited in order to punish Palestinians, who had nothing to do with them. There is a movement to take Israeli schoolchildren to visit Auschwitz and other Nazi concentration camps, and some children have been so confused by the messages they have been given that they blame the Palestinians for the Holocaust.

The world could be made more aware of Israel's injustices by a new breed of Palestinian political leaders who spent more time promoting the huge merits of the Palestinian case to the world rather than playing power politics among different factions. Instead of clinging to the Two State solution, playing

[23] https://forward.com/opinion/394094/young-jews-are-actually-winning-the-generational-war-over-israel/?utm_content=daily_Newsletter_MainList_Title_Position-1&utm_source=Sailthru&utm_medium=email&utm_campaign=Daily%20-%20M-Th%202018-02-14&utm_term=The%20Forward%20Today%20Monday-Friday

into Israeli hands, new leaders could actively promote One Democratic State in Palestine. It is a mystery to me why the Two State solution has survived so long. In a recent poll more than 53% of Palestinians believed that a Two State Solution was no longer viable. I'm surprised the figure is so low. It is *clearly* no longer viable.

Do such new political leaders exist? I am convinced that they do. I even know one or two, but they have no interest in entering the fray until the current Palestinian Authority/Hamas division breaks down and new lines of allegiance are drawn which neither call for the destruction of Israel nor kowtow to Israel for the sake of being allowed to stay in power.

• An 'intifada' event

The Palestinians have fought two popular street-based resistance movements. Each of them has shocked Israel into realising that the Palestinians were not going to put up forever with its oppressive policies. And of course, these intifadas have drawn worldwide attention to the Palestinians' plight, as well as adding a new word to world languages. But there is no shortage of smaller resistance activities which take place weekly in the towns and village of the Occupied Territories. Any one of the groups, from family-sized upwards, which organise these demonstrations and protests could suddenly do something which happens to inspire Palestinians in other locations, attract media attention, irritate the Israeli government, challenge the settlements or the existence of the Wall, or generate another 'Ahed Tamimi' moment. I even heard of a scheme involving catapults and 'tetraprongs', four-pronged devices with sharpened points easily made in any garage, to be projected on to the apartheid roads that join the settlements, puncturing the tyres of every car that drove on those roads. Not ultimate victory, but at least a sign of Palestinian control over their own territory.

One should not underestimate the potential of unplanned, individually-motivated actions in changing world politics. The fall of the Berlin Wall began with events in two other countries, Hungary and Austria, when East German tourists refused to return home and escaped into Austria after the Hungarian government dismantled an electric fence. In the same year, a rousing speech by a Romanian priest set in motion a series of events which led to the Romanian revolution and the downfall of Ceausescu. Now, these events were more destructive than constructive. There were no plans for a new situation but to destroy an old one. In the case of Israel and Palestine, however the transition to a single state happens, it will be more a more positive change than the bugbear created by the Israelis of 'pushing the Jews into the sea.' (If you want to know what pushing people into the sea is really like, you should read about what happened to the Arab inhabitants of Jaffa during the 1948 Arab-Israeli War.)

Of course, the problem with this sort of scenario – the concatenation of a series of unconnected but significant events – is that they cannot be organised to happen. But if unprecedented turmoil, accompanied by the realisation that things have gone far enough, does occur, the merits of the One State Solution, promising a state of peace between the Jews and the Arabs of Palestine will start to seem not just attractive but the least worst situation for the next century in the Middle East.

One final point, because I know you've been wondering. What will the state be called? Here's a suggestion:

Taking a leaf from the single state of Trinidad and Tobago, it could be called Palestine and Israel. Or Israel and Palestine. Or Israel/Palestine or Palestine/Israel interchangeably. Or using the Swiss model, where German-, Italian- and French-speaking Swiss each talk about their country with a different name, it could be called 'Palestine' by its Arab inhabitants and 'Israel' by the Jews. Or, on the model of the United Arab Republic, a shortlived union between Syria and Egypt, it could be called the 'United Semitic Republic'. (When a theatre company in the new state put on a performance of Shakespeare's *Antony and Cleopatra*, the line "I am dying, Egypt, dying" had to be changed to "I am dying, Southern Region of the United Arab Republic, dying.")

The one suggestion I would not adopt was that suggested by the late Muammar al-Gaddafi, who favoured the One-State Solution but thought the new nation should be called 'Isratine'. Somehow that sounds more like a type of nutty chocolate confection than the name of a state which, given a fair wind and a trillion dollars, could bring peace, stability and a new vitality to the Middle East.

12   Epilogue

From *The Guardian*, May 15th, 2022
Guardian correspondents and agency staff

There were extraordinary scenes in Palestine-Israel yesterday, a national holiday and the first day of the new state's existence. From the Jordan to the Mediterranean people woke up with a feeling of freedom. Everyone could now visit any part of what had been Israel and the Occupied Territories. Arabs in Jericho or Ramallah could drive or get the bus to Jaffa; Jews in Tel Aviv or Haifa could now visit what they liked to call Judaea and Samaria. Overnight, the roads of the West Bank had lost their network of checkpoints, or rather the military posts were still there but there were no soldiers, and the barriers all rose symbolically in the air, as if to say 'feel free to pass through'.

In the former Israeli settlements, many on hilltops with barbed wire fences lying dismantled on the ground, Jewish settlers looked out warily as Arab villagers from the valleys below, whose land had been taken by Israel, strolled up the hill and along the well-kept streets of the settlement, pointed out to their children the playgrounds and swimming pools, and waved at the settlers, calling out 'Welcome' in Arabic. While some settlers sat sullenly on their verandas, others walked tentatively towards the Arabs and shook hands or patted children on the head. A few even brought cold drinks.

But it was in the former territory of Israel that the most extraordinary scenes were played out. From early morning, streams of cars crisscrossed Israel-Palestine bringing some former residents of Arab towns and villages to places they hadn't seen for seventy years, and their children and grandchildren to places they had only ever heard talked about in hushed but defiant terms by their parents and grandparents. Some knocked on the doors of Arab stone houses long occupied by Jews from Russia and Germany and America and were welcomed by the current residents. A new law of reconciliation, enshrined in the Palestine-Israel constitution, encouraged tenants and owners of former Arab homes to let any Arab with a connection with the house look around the former family home. In the longer term, there are also financial incentives – but no compulsion – for them to move out to make way for Arabs who might like to live there. This scheme has been compared to the subsidies and payments which were given to the former Israeli settlers to encourage them to move to the West Bank.

At the main airport, formerly Ben-Gurion airport, now renamed Judah Magnes airport after the Jewish academic who favoured the One State Solution in the 1930s, a succession of A380 aircraft landed during the day, each bringing 600 lucky returners who had won tickets in a ballot to attend the first day celebrations.

There were new sights to be seen everywhere. Members of the new police force, a mixed force of Jews and Arabs, did their best to control the traffic flows, but there were major traffic jams all over the new state. The biggest were in the south, around Gaza, where the demolition of the fence hemming in the inhabitants had been carried out over the previous week, with strict instructions to the Gazans not to cross the border until P-I Day. From midnight last night, cars streamed out from all the roads in Gaza, mainly to the north but some heading to villages and towns in the south, from where many of the refugees had come. The road from Gaza to Ashkelon, Jaffa, Tel Aviv and the north was jammed solid, even though, for the day, traffic was one way north in both lanes. All along the road, in anticipation of the long delays, government-funded refreshment stalls offered free drinks and hummus to the waiting passengers.

In Tel Aviv, a city which had seen few Arab visitors and no Arab residents, the main streets and beach side roads were thronged with curious Palestinians. Some had parked at large temporary car parks outside Tel Aviv and Jaffa its southern neighbour, and used park and ride buses to visit the two towns. The attitude of the visitors from the former Occupied Territories was mainly curiosity. But in Jaffa, there were emotional scenes as former residents sought out their houses and homes. Many wept as they discovered large paved-over parks and recreational areas where closely-packed Arab houses had been destroyed, either before 1948 by the British or after by the Israelis attempting to 'judaise' the town.

Everywhere, official signs carried the name of the new state. Signs in Israel had always been bilingual, although it was more of a novelty in the Occupied Territories. The main difference was the new flag, a combination of triangles reflecting the former Palestinian and Israeli flags without reproducing either.

Everywhere there were road signs to the sites of destroyed villages in what was Israel. In the past, the locations of these villages had often been concealed. Many of them had left no trace, other than the ring of prickly pear plants that protected many villages and which clung stubbornly to the site seventy years after the village had disappeared. Now, their locations were heralded by large signs and newly built roads to take former residents and their descendants to special visitor centres with maps and photographs telling the history of those villages and giving the names of the people who lived there.

Small family groups walked around in a daze, hardly believing that Palestine was one again. Often, elderly people kissed the ground while younger family members looked on, a little embarrassed.

In the Galilee, the area still most like the old pre-1948 Palestine, most of the traffic came from Lebanon and Syria, through borders now opened after having been closed for decades. In every village there were banners across the road, welcoming parties, tables set up with food and drink, and stages for official greetings from mayors and dabka dancing by locals. In many villages there were reunions between people who had been able to stay in the village in 1948 and their relatives who had been expelled by the Israelis, or left to avoid the conflict and were barred from returning.

Many of the visitors, from camps over the border, had lived for decades a few miles from their ancestral villages but had been unable to visit. Some were too poor to afford cars but thanks to a massive operation by the Jordanian, Lebanese and Syrian governments, luxury coaches crossed the borders in a carefully scheduled operation designed to bring a million refugees into Israel-Palestine during the first week of the new state, to visit their former homes. For many of them, eventually as part of the Right of Return programme, they will return permanently, to newly built villages near to their original homes.

The most extraordinary scenes took place in Jerusalem. In the Old City, of course, many Palestinians returned to the Haram al-Sherif or the Holy Sepulchre. Whether or not their families had lived there, this was a place of pilgrimage from which many had been banned. But there were also crowds of returning Palestinians in West Jerusalem, some there to gawp at the ubiquitous evidence that this was no longer the capital of a Jewish state, merely of one in which Jews and Arabs lived. Ambitious plans had been published to make houses in some of the formerly Arab suburbs of Jerusalem available to returning Palestinians, and groups toured the streets looking at fine examples of 1920-30s domestic architecture.

At the former Israeli Knesset building, now the parliament of Palestine-Israel, all religious symbols had been stripped out, and reconstruction work in the main chamber was under way to install the increased number of members' seats needed for the enlarged parliament, yet to be elected.

In the late afternoon, crowds began to drift towards the centre of the Old City, beneath the wall built by Suleiman the Magnificent. A stage had been set up in the plaza, and seats filled the space, with tiers rising on the far side. There had been a ballot for citizens of the new state to attend the dedication ceremony, equal numbers of Jews and Arabs, and they were already in their seats as the sun began to set. Then, at 8 p.m. coaches carrying world leaders began to arrive at the side gate, and there was applause from the crowds for the first coachload, carrying the people who had been most active in supporting the reunification of Palestine and Israel. President Winfrey of the USA, Prime Minister Corbyn, leaders of the Quartet, the Secretary General of the UN, and three philanthropists who between them had started off the Reunification Fund, the Koch Brothers and George Soros. Although on opposite sides of the political spectrum, these three were seen later to join hands for the national anthem.

On one side, closely flanked by police officers, the former prime minister of Israel, Binyamin Netanyahu, sat with a stony expression on his face.

At 9 p.m. the co-Presidents-elect of Palestine-Israel, Mustafa Barghouti and Ilan Pappé appeared on the platform to tumultuous applause. The speaker of the House, an Armenian Palestinian, Albert Aghazarian, tossed a coin to see who would speak first. Co-President Bargouti called 'heads' but it was tails, so co-President Pappé stood up to give the first speech.

There was a shout of acclamation as Pappé, a Jew, started to speak in Arabic. There was no interpreter, since both co-Presidents made the same speech, each welcoming the citizens of the new state from Jewish or Arab backgrounds. When co-President Barghouti stood up to speak, he too received applause as soon as he started to speak in Hebrew.

The most extraordinary thing about the day was the absence of animosity between former Israelis and exiled Palestinians. This was partly because, months ago, many Jews who were fanatically opposed to the reunification had left Israel to return to their countries of origin, helped with a large translocation grant. Most of these were Russians, and many of them were not even Jews but had emigrated to Israel under loosened rules designed to increase the population of Israel. There were also small numbers of Palestinian militants who were deemed to be a possible threat and they were closely watched by the joint Arab-Jewish security forces.

One other factor played a role in the comparative peacefulness of this significant day. Many Israelis who might have voted for successive right-wing governments because they believed the racist arguments about the Palestinians had had two years to come to terms with the proposed existence of the new state, and had been strongly influenced by the final pro-peace government of Israel tasked with ensuring a smooth transition. Measures to create a sense of shared citizenship by prearranged meetings between groups of Palestinians and Israelis led to some Israelis meeting Palestinians for the first time even though the population of Israel had been 20% Palestinian Arab. A transitional year in Israel and the Occupied Territories where everyone shared the same bi-lingual and bi-cultural television channels and print media had also projected a picture that was very different from the all-out violence predicted by opponents of the One-State Solution.

Perhaps the message that most reinforced the hopefulness that was everywhere on the first day of the new state was the realisation that, even with the huge amounts of money needed to reunify the state and put into action a major Right of Return programme, economists were already predicting unprecedented prosperity for the new state, not so much from the large amounts of promised aid from the rest of the world which, in any case, would be phased out over the next ten years, but from the earning power and savings of the returning Palestinians, and the huge increases in construction work, the retail sector, the financial services sector and tourism.

The co-Presidents finished their prepared speech with the following words:

"In decades to come, our children and grandchildren, as well as historians and politicians in the rest of the world, will look at what we have done today and say 'Why did it take so long?'"

The tumultuous applause, mixed with the ululations of Palestinian women, lasted more than fifteen minutes, and the two co-Presidents had great difficulty getting off the stage as they responded to the multitudes of hands held up from the audience to be shaken at this historic moment.

Appendix 1

One step forward which might start the ball rolling is a UN General Assembly resolution laying out some principles for the setting up of the new state. It has been drawn up after consultation with a number of academics and a former member of the UK delegation to the UN.

Resolution
Israel/Palestine and the establishment of a unified secular democratic state

The General Assembly,

Guided by the principles of the Charter of the United Nations,

Considering that the territory occupied by the state of Israel was formerly the Mandatory territory of Palestine, with a population of Arabs and Jews who shared the rights of habitation and of self-determination, and that the establishment of the state of Israel in 1948 and the occupation of further territories in 1967 were accomplished against the wishes of the Palestinians

Recognizing also that the state of Israel as currently constituted is a de jure racially defined state in which Jewish citizens enjoy preferential treatment over non-Jewish ones;

Recalling its resolutions GA194 (1948) on the repatriation of the Palestinian refugees displaced in the hostilities of 1948-9, and GA273 (III) 1949, admitting Israel as a member of the United Nations on Israel's willingness to carry out the obligations of the UN Charter and 'to honour them from the day of its acceptance', including Resolutions 181 and 194,

Recalling also relevant Security Council resolutions on the illegality of settlement building and the status of Jerusalem; and the declaration by the International Court of Justice of the illegality of the construction of a wall in the Occupied Palestinian Territory,

Aware that Israeli settlement activities involve, inter alia, the transfer of nationals of the occupying Power into the occupied territories, the confiscation of land, the exploitation of natural resources and other illegal actions against the Palestinian civilian population,

Reaffirming the applicability of the Geneva Convention relative to the Protection of Civilian Persons in Time of War, of 12 August 1949, to the Occupied Palestinian Territory, including East Jerusalem,

Reiterating its opposition to settlement activities in the Occupied Palestinian Territory, including East Jerusalem, and to any activities involving the confiscation of land, the disruption of the livelihood of protected persons and the de facto annexation of land,

Recalling the need to end all acts of violence between the parties,

Gravely concerned about the dangerous situation resulting from actions taken by the illegal armed Israeli settlers in the occupied territory,

Noting Israel's non-compliance with repeated attempts to arrive at a negotiated settlement to the conflict, including, UNSC Resolutions 242 (1967) and 338 (1973), the Oslo Accords (1993), and the Road Map (2002);

Taking note of the relevant reports of the Secretary-General, and of the recent report in May 2007 of the Special Rapporteur of the Human Rights Council on the situation of human rights in the Palestinian territories occupied by Israel since 1967,

Recognising that Israel has on a number of occasions claimed and sought to acquire the whole territory of Mandate Palestine;

Recognising also that the Palestinians have sought and

have a right to continue to live in, or to return to, cities, towns, villages and communities that they and their families have inhabited for generations, in accordance with international law;

Recognising also that Israeli citizens, aided by the government of Israel, have illegally built communities and settlements which, in spite of the illegality, they wish to continue to inhabit:

Calls upon representatives of Israel and Palestine to agree on behalf of their peoples to share the land between the Mediterranean and the river Jordan, currently divided between Israel, the West Bank and Gaza, by setting up a state which is democratic and secular, in which the rights of all people living within its borders to freedom of worship, security from violence and equality under the law are enshrined in a new constitution, to replace the separate government instruments that apply currently in Israel, the West Bank and Gaza.

Calls upon the new state to ensure that per capita expenditure on public services, education, transport, health and local authorities is applied impartially to all citizens, regardless of creed;

Requires the new state of Israel/Palestine (or whatever name its constitution shall finally determine) to abide by the provisions of the United Nations Charter;

Offers the offices of the United Nations to all parties to the dispute to host an interim constitutional conference to draw up heads of agreement covering a new parliamentary structure, legislative and executive structures, foreign relations and citizenship redefinitions for the new state;

Requires all parties to participate in a Border Dismantling and Redefining Committee, with the following brief:

1. To schedule the removal of the illegal wall currently constructed on Palestinian land,

2. To ensure free passage on all public roads in the new state to all citizens,

3. To remove all security fences and armed guards from every housing estate or community, to allow free access

for all citizens of the new state;

4. To enact new land laws that apply equally and fairly to all citizens of the new state;

5. To ensure the equitable sharing of resources, including water;

6. To respect the special status of Jerusalem in regard to its unique importance for the three main religions by instituting an appropriate administration for the holy places;

Demands that the new state abide by Strategic Arms Limitation Treaties, banning the holding or development of nuclear weapons;

Calls upon the world community to support the efforts of all parties to establish the new state, with economic assistance and expert advice;

Emphasizes the strong will of the world community to put every effort into the one-state solution of this intractable problem;

Recognises the recent efforts made by regional and international parties to resolve the conflict through the creation of two states;

Recommends the adoption of this or any other agreed arrangement, including federation and binationalism, provided these are adopted as interim stages in the attainment of the one-state solution, and provided they do not hinder this end result;

Requests the Secretary-General to report to the General Assembly at its seventy-sixth session on the implementation of the present resolution.

Appendix 2

An alternative 'Balfour Declaration' for the 21st century

Foreign Office
November 2nd, 2018

Dear Mr Abbas,

I have much pleasure in conveying to you, on behalf of Her Majesty's Government, the following declaration of sympathy with Palestinian Arab aspirations which has been submitted to, and approved by, the Cabinet

His Majesty's government view with favour the establishment in Israel and Palestine of a national home for the Palestinian people, and will use their best endeavours to facilitate the achievement of this object, it being clearly understood that nothing shall be done which may prejudice the civil and religious rights of existing non-Arab communities in Israel and Palestine, or the rights and political status enjoyed by Arabs in any other country.

I should be grateful if you would bring this declaration to the knowledge of the Palestinian National Council.

Yours,

*Secretary of State for
Foreign and Commonwealth
Affairs*

Appendix 3

As part of its continuing efforts to demonstrate the feasibility of Palestinians returning to their home villages, the Palestine Land Society has a multiphase competition for architects and planners to show how they would reconstruct 500 of the villages destroyed by Israel in 1948-9. The village that was the subject of the winning entry in 2017 was Tantoura, a village forcibly 'cleansed' of its inhabitants by the Israeli army and then demolished.

■ EXISTING MASSING
▨ OLD VILLAGE MASSING
▧ PROPOSED MASSING

Further reading

Anglo-Arab Relations and the Question of Palestine, 1914-21, A.L. Tibawi, Luzac, 1977

Balfour in the Dock, Colin Andersen, Skyscraper Publications, 2017

In Search of Fatima, Ghada Karmi, Verso, 2009

Married to Another Man, Ghada Karmi, Pluto, 2007

Nisi Dominus, Nevill Barbour, Harrap, 1946

Palestine: A Personal History, Karl Sabbagh, Atlantic Books, 2006

Palestine: The Reality, J.M.N. Jeffries, Skyscraper Publications, 2017

Politically Incorrect, Ofra Yeshua-Lyth, Skyscraper Publications, 2017

The Ethnic Cleansing of Palestine, Ilan Pappé, Oneworld, 2007

The Invention of the Jewish People, Shlomo Sand, Verso, 2010

The One-State Solution, Virginia Tilley, Manchester University Press, 2005